*He looked at his own Soul
with a Telescope. What seemed
all irregular, he saw and
shewed to be beautiful
Constellations; and he added
to the Consciousness hidden
worlds within worlds.*

—Coleridge

This Hopi symbol depicts the human condition. The maze can be read as the unknown territory through which man must find his way in this life. It is also a Medicine Wheel, with the small clear quadrant where the human figure stands representing the person's Starting Place, and the remainder of the maze being those human traits that man must pursue to be whole.

"Man In A Maze," by Susan Ida Smith.

Inner Guides
VISIONS
DREAMS
& *Dr. Einstein*

Hal Zina Bennett, Ph.D.

CELESTIALARTS

Berkeley, California

Celestial Arts
P.O. Box 7327
Berkeley, California 94707

This is a "Field Guides to Inner Resources" book, a series of tools for tapping the wealth of our inner worlds.

Cover and book design by Ken Scott
Typesetting by Ann Flanagan Typography

Manufactured in the United States of America
First Printing, 1986

Library of Congress Cataloging-in-Publication Data

Bennett, Hal Zina, 1936–
    Inner guides, visions, dreams & Dr. Einstein.
    Bibliography: p.
    Includes index.
    1. Spirits—Miscellanea. 2. Visions—Miscellanea.
3. Dreams—Miscellanea. I. Title. II. Title: Inner
guides, visions, dreams, and Dr. Einstein.
BF1999.B3957 1986   131   86-13004
ISBN 0-89087-464-6

1 2 3 4 5 6 7 8 9 0 — 90 89 88 87

By the same author:

Mind Jogger
The Doctor Within
Spirit Guides: Access to Inner Worlds
(with Mike Samuels, M.D.)
The Well Body Book
(with Mike Samuels, M.D.)
Well Body, Well Earth
(with Mike Samuels, M.D.)
Peak Performance
(with Charles Garfield)

ACKNOWLEDGEMENTS

Thanks David Hinds and Paul Reed for your support, suggestions and attention to detail that helped bring this book to its present form. Thanks Ken Scott for your fine book design, as attractive as it is appropriate and Ann Flanagan for flawless typography. My special gratitude to the many people at Celestial Arts/Ten Speed whose names don't appear herein but who have played important parts in giving this book its life. Thank you George Young for humor and wisdom. And thanks, Phil, for the vision and fortitude that built this wonderful playground and publishing venture.

With much love,
I dedicate this book to my son Nathan,
on his 23rd birthday.

TABLE OF CONTENTS

Inner Guides, Visions, Dreams & Dr. Einstein

I magine a meeting between the American mathematician Albert Einstein, the Swiss psychoanalyst Carl Jung, the Jesuit paleontologist Teilhard de Chardin, and Poshaiankia, who in Zuni mythology is the Father of the medicine societies. Their meeting takes place on the screen of my consciousness. It is as though certain of their key ideas have reproduced their whole beings in my mind.

In holographic theory, any one piece of the holographic film, though only a remnant, can reproduce a three-dimensional likeness of the whole. And I can't help but wonder, can it be that ideas are like this—fragments that have the capacity to produce mental holograms, invoking the presence of the person who originally expressed the idea? If the whole person is not reproduced in this way, at least the spirit of their thought may be.

The holograms of these people are here in my mind because I have asked them to help me explore the nature of the human consciousness, its geography, its climates, its relationships with other consciousnesses.

For a moment I look inward and see my entire consciousness as a vast landscape, stretching out into space, a space that appears to have no beginning, middle or end. This vast landscape has an identity all its own, with hills and trees and people and cities and machines, even skies and planets and stars, yet there is the clear sense that it mingles with other consciousnesses, billions of them, sharing borders, sharing events.

For each of us, our consciousness is much like a planet, teeming with life, peopled with figures who move and talk, who love and hate, who are creative and destructive, people who, in short, behave very much as our friends and acquaintances behave.

Jung says: "There are things in the psyche which I do not produce, but which produce themselves and have their own life. My own anima figure, Philemon, represented a force which was not myself. In my fantasies I held conversations with him, and he said things which I had not consciously thought. He said I treated thoughts as if I generated them myself, but in his view, thoughts were like animals in the forest, or people in a room, or birds in the air. He told me, 'If you were to meet some people in a room, you would not think that you had made those people, or that you were responsible for the judgements they made or the things they said, or the ways they lived their lives.' Philemon was a mysterious figure for me. I went walking in the garden with him, and he was for me what the Indians call a guru."

I wonder, "Is there any true separation between our inner worlds and the outer, or is that separation just an illusion that we somehow find comfort in maintaining?"

Now, on the screen of my consciousness, I see Einstein. He appears to be listening to my thoughts, thoughts that I never actually stated aloud. At last he says, "I can only answer that in terms of what I know of the physical world. If we are anywhere near seeing the truth in science, we know that the movement of each elemental particle in the universe will affect and be affected by the movements of every other, that each is sensitive to the other, regardless of what form each is taking or where it is located in space and time. As a scientist we must look at man himself in the same way.

"We ourselves are made of the same stuff—assembled from these elemental particles that make up all matter in the universe, recycled billions of times over, in billions of different forms. We see that even our thoughts, which are biochemical events in which the participating particles are subject to the same physical laws I have described, will affect the Universe as a whole. For the nuclear physicist this is of particular interest because it means that we cannot even *observe* a single seemingly isolated phenomenon without changing that phenomenon, no matter how *objective* or *un-meddling* we might try to be. At best we can only assume that what we are observing is how that material behaves when it is being observed by us."

Chardin has been listening with rapt attention. When Einstein is done he says: "If the universe is as interactive and interdependent as you describe, then the religious concept of being *at one with the universe* is not simply a theological question, it is a physical reality. Every person, every rock, every flea acts upon and is acted upon by every other. Our belief in a broad set of connections, eternal bonds between the Earth and all it contains and God is not Faith alone but a physical reality."

"All of us evolved from the same cosmic egg, and so we are connected forever," Einstein says, nodding to show his agreement with Chardin.

"It did not begin where you think it did," Poshaiankia interjects. "The Universe you describe begins with mass and energy. But spirit began long before that. My cosmology begins with the Nothingness, the Void, and in this Nothingness there was neither mass, nor space, nor time, nor energy, nor anything else that man's mind finds easy and comfortable to perceive. But in that Nothingness was the Maker, who is not any of these—not mass, not space, not time, not energy. The Maker made the cosmic egg—the source of all of these—but the Maker is not *of* these. Human life *is of these.*

"Human life has form, and humans believe in that form. And, because they believe in that, they can once again touch the Maker only if they trick themselves, shedding the material self—the form—for a moment. Mathematics gives us one trick for doing this, but there are many other tricks, tricks that the shaman perfected long before modern physics, tricks that play the limits of man's own form against itself, breaking its self-imposed boundaries so that he may leap outside the illusion of his material self."

Carl Jung nods thoughtfully. His face lights up, and, with what might be described as a mischievous grin, he says: "So the theologian and the scientist speak the same language at last—but they do it through the aborigine!"

Einstein and Chardin chuckle to themselves.

"I am fascinated by Mr. Einstein," Poshaiankia says. "He has seen what my people could not see without his scientific tools. Within our belief system, the most elemental things in the universe are also the most powerful. So we believe that rock and the flow of the rivers and the wind and lightning are the most powerful because they are the most eternal, the closest to the Maker. And so the elemental particles, of which Mr. Einstein speaks, are perhaps the most powerful, and the closest to the Maker, of all."

"You bring up an interesting point," Einstein tells Poshaiankia. "To claim that man's spirit is not subject to the laws of quantum physics seems to me as inappropriate a response as the Church refusing to accept Galileo's evidence that the sun, not the earth, was the center of our galaxy. My scientific associate Ludwig Boltzmann says that only when we see the human spirit and will as parts of the body, existing because of the evolution of the physico-chemical forces (which you will remember are only ordered collections of elemental particles) can we have a complete picture of the human experience."

Jung is obviously excited by this statement. His expression is pensive for a moment; then he says: "You provide me with an excellent rationale for my view of synchronicity, or acausal relationships between events. So often I experienced it in my life, in patients who made transferences to me, or with those who were emotionally very close to me. We might be separated by hundreds of miles, yet I would have an experience which would be similar to one they were having, often at the same time. Once, while on a lecture tour, I awakened in my hotel room with a start and had the distinct impression that someone had quickly entered and then left my room. I turned on the light, but no one was there. I checked, and neither was there anyone in the hallway. Then I became aware of a dull pain, as though something had struck my forehead and then the back of my skull. I later learned that at that same hour, in a city many miles away, a patient of mine had committed suicide. He had shot himself in the forehead, and the bullet had lodged in the back of his skull.

"If what you say about the responsiveness of elemental particles is true, it could explain the mechanism that makes this kind of synchronicity possible. This also suggests that the archetypes that take on lives in our unconscious have physical realities of a very particular sort, and that they may be transmitted from person to person not only through direct teachings but also through the *ether,* if you will, through the swirls of assembled particles that form the noosphere, as Chardin calls it. Is not Chardin's noosphere, after all, shaped by the collective consciousness of all experience since the beginning of time?"

Chardin nods but does not speak.

Poshaiankia studies Jung's face for a moment, then says: "It is out of what you call this ether, these clouds of particles that swirl around the Universe, that *all* thought and all form comes. These swirls, the greatest of the Maker's mysteries, are the source of all knowing. Each person may reach into these swirls with his own imperfect knowledge, his own image of truth, and gather greater wisdom, wisdom that, if trusted, will carry him closer and closer to the Maker. But we need all our tricks, our inner spirits and our visions and our fetiches and, yes our mathematics and science and religions to do this."

"Is not our Earth like some great body which is being born," Chardin reflects, "with its limbs, its nervous system, its perceptive organs, its memory—the body, in fact, of that great Thing which had to come to fulfill the ambitions aroused in the reflective being by the newly acquired consciousness that he was at one with and responsible to an evolutionary All?"

"The psyche or unconscious, as I see it," Jung adds, "must be our greatest personal connection with the noosphere, since it is through the unconscious that we are connected with the symbolism of truth that has belonged to mankind for eons."

"We must reserve space in our thoughts for the Unknowable," Poshaiankia says. "It is not simply for ourselves, or for the Earth, or for the Universe, but for the Unknowable that we must choose our thoughts and deeds."

Jung nods emphatically.

Poshaiankia continues: "That is why the medicine of talking to the spirits is such a great source of power for all of us, even for modern man. Our thoughts and the thoughts of our grandfathers move like ripples on a pond throughout the Unknowable. There is nothing that can resist the collective force of our spirit beings when we empower them by giving them space in our minds.

"Furthermore, we have a very real duty to perform for this great consciousness. It is not that we must learn ways to cause our unconscious or psyche, as Dr. Jung calls it, to serve our consciousness. It is the other way around. Each of our psyches are nothing more than grains of thought in the Unknowable. Our outer lives—the actions we take in the world where our bodies live and breath and move—are only there to serve the inner world. Man must take his lead from his inner world, his unconscious, and have his actions and thoughts be true to it. That is the duty of us all, to live our outer lives in the service of our inner lives and thus in the service of the Unknowable."

Einstein says: "For many years my fellow scientists were annoyed by my contention that imagination—that which occurs within our minds—was more important than knowledge. But here we have a perfect example of the importance of this. Imagination may well be our greatest link with Nature, with our Universe. Without that link we are limited to the finite experience of our material beings.

"It is only when we are silent, giving imagination full reign, that we receive the knowledge assembled in what Poshaiankia calls the Unknowable, or which Chardin calls the noosphere, and which Dr. Jung might call the *collective unconscious* of our planet."

"It is clearly time to stop pretending that this planet, our own consciousness—which we touch only with our thoughts and feelings, only with our spirits—does not have a profound affect on the world that we perceive with our senses," Chardin says. "Each of these worlds is as a single cell in a great brain, a single idea or image in a vast consciousness. We are participants, just as each cell of a living organism is a participant, in a larger whole that we can only imagine.

"The idea is that of the Earth not only becoming covered by myriads of grains of thought, but becoming enclosed in a single thinking envelope, so as to form, functionally, no more than a single vast grain of thought on the sidereal scale, the plurality of individual experiences grouping together and reinforcing one another in the act of a single unanimous reflection."

The conference stops here. For the moment, the vast inner landscape fades and narrows for me, and I am aware once more of my body and the everyday limits of my mind. I sit in front of the computer, where I have been recording all this, and am aware once again of the amber lights forming words on the dark field of the CRT.

I press buttons on the keyboard, shifting the text up and down, scanning the electronic memory which now holds all that I have described here. As I do so, I reflect on the conference I have recorded. Perhaps, influenced by the linear process of operating the computer, I become more logical and practical.

I am fully aware of the fact that all that has taken place here has been an illusion. These teachers—these participants in the imaginary conference—have given me much to think about, connecting my life with the lives of others on this planet. I feel a call to join with others who are helping to make experiences of our inner worlds accessible to an ever greater number of people.

Until the past two decades, techniques for getting to know the inner world, to travel safely within it, have been in the hands of an elite—the priest, the Oracle, the guru, the shaman, and more recently the psychologist.

We are living in a time of vast change, a time when greater and greater numbers of people are asking for information and tools to expand their understanding and mastery of their own inner worlds. In the Reformation of the sixteenth century, mankind claimed and won the right to *private judgement* in interpreting the Bible. Now the struggle is quieter and subtler, without violence, and often without public fanfare, but no less important than what happened 400 years ago. As Marilyn Ferguson has pointed out in her book *The Aquarian Conspiracy,* it is a revolution "whose roots are old and deep in human history, (and which) belongs to all of us." As her work has clearly shown, we are claiming and winning our rights to private judgements about our own inner worlds.

This little book you hold in your hand opens one small window onto this vast and exciting inner world, providing a few simple tools for working more intimately and more in harmony with the peopled landscape that you will find within you.

CHAPTER ONE:

The Adventure Inward

The inner world of human consciousness has always been the source of our greatest survival powers and our greatest achievements as a species. It is out of this that we have created so much—great cities, great works of technology and art, and more recently, the ability to understand basic energy principles of the universe. And yet, many people are fearful of their inner world—as though it were an ominous territory, filled with unpredictable and uncontrollable possibilities. The fact that we already live most of our lives within that world does not occur to most of us. We actually know that world quite well. Without it, we wouldn't be able to perform the simplest act.

Even for the most timid inner world adventurers, there is a certain familiarity about the territory. Like tourists who have been there only to visit, we know the streets and are accustomed to the faces and dress of the people we meet there. But we still feel distant, foreigners suffering from a kind of language barrier, ignorant of the customs, and this keeps us from participating at the level we might wish to participate.

But why should we *want* to participate in this inner world? What benefits can we possibly enjoy from such a venture? The specific benefits that each individual might reap are, or course, impossible to name. But in a general way we know that only by having access to this inner world can the individual expand awareness and realize his or her true potential. This potential may be realized in relationships, in emotional and physical well-being, in greater prosperity, in having an increased ability to face problems and find solutions in everyday life, in creative endeavors, and in tapping into the powers of what some people call the sixth sense, and which others call intuition, or even psychic abilities.

I have always felt that my greatest journeys were not taken in automobiles or airplanes or trains or boats, transporting me over the countryside or across the water or the sky, but in vehicles made of mind stuff, transporting me through the inner world. For me, the inner world has always seemed filled with limitless possibilities. I have to agree with the psychologist C. G. Jung that this inner world is "the greatest of all cosmic wonders." By comparison, as exciting and fulfilling as it can be, the external world seems filled with frustrating restrictions.

The trouble with the inner world is that there are no hard landmarks, which—like the walls of the houses we live in or the buildings where we work—allow us to use our senses of touch or smell or sight to cross-check our perceptions. Most of us live in a world where only that which can be confirmed with our sensory receptors seems "real." It is clear to us all that the automobile, or the microwave oven, or books or bombs began as pure mindstuff, and only later were given physical realities. And it is clear that love, or anger or sadness that originate in one person's mind, can alter the way others around them feel and behave. Yet, for most people, the stuff of the inner world, where all these are born, remains a shadowy dreamlike space that is only remotely related to their daily lives. How hard it is to convince ourselves that what goes on in the mind is "real!"

There are two key experiences in my life that ultimately guided me towards greater trust of that inner world. The first event occurred when, during an illness (Tularemia) as a teenager, I was hospitalized with an extremely high fever and went into a deep coma. A part of me was fully aware and awake during this time, and I vividly remember the experience of traveling freely in my inner world, excited by the prospect of exploring it endlessly.

I recall clearly how, in my mind, I traveled down a long tube or tunnel, like a spiral of energy and light, and near the end of that tube I saw a vast opening into an area I cannot adequately describe. It is not that my vision of that space is unclear; rather, it is truly impossible to find words to describe it. The closest I can come is "infinite space," or "space without form." But since words are themselves finite, the experience in the *infinite* that I had eludes my definition. I can only say that there was consciousness and awareness of a sort, but even that appeared to take no form I have experienced before or since.

As I entered this space I was aware that I had a choice between going back to my physical body—it lay in the hospital bed packed in a plastic body bag filled with ice to lower my fever—or leaving it forever. My consciousness appeared to be separated from my body. I remember looking down from a vantage point that would have put me somewhere in the center of the hospital room above mine. It was not like having x-ray vision, where you see through physical forms. Rather, as I experienced it, space and time were completely maleable, like illusions that could be shifted about at will, as in high resolution computer graphics.

I saw my father sitting in a chair by my bedside. It was around two o'clock in the morning, and he had been called there by the doctors who had told him that I might not last through the night. He was crying, very alone in his grief. As I looked at him, I became aware that he had protected my mother from the distressing message the doctors had given him. At the time, my mother was also ill, hospitalized elsewhere with a gall bladder problem.

As I watched this scene I began to feel sorry for my father, and maybe a little guilty for even entertaining the idea of not returning to my body. When I decided to come back, I think my decision was based as much on my desire to comfort my father as anything else. The prospect of dying, of going on into that limitless space I perceived, was in no way threatening. I remember reflecting about the fear of death and thinking how totally unfounded it was. Death itself was not at all what it is made out to be.

The next day, my fever broke, and I began a long struggle back to the living. I discovered that it wasn't going to be easy. My muscles had atrophied, and I hadn't even the strength to stand by myself. I had lost over forty pounds, leaving me literally skin and bones. I had lost nearly all the hair on my body, and what was most shocking of all, I had lost my sight. I saw only light and dark. The world had become little more than a shadow show behind a filmy grey screen.

On the surface, my rehabilitation took three or four months. In that time, I regained my strength, my body hair grew back, and my sight was restored, though I had to wear glasses. Life itself had changed, however. Nothing looked quite the same for me again. Thoughts, ideas, even the way I viewed the physical world—all had undergone alterations that at times bewildered me. I recall looking at objects that I had always taken so much for granted—like houses and rocks and flowers—and seeing them in an entirely new light. They were no longer simple, separate objects in the world. I perceived that the border where a tree became sky, for example, was nothing more than a shift in the assembly of particles of energy. I knew nothing about quantum physics at this time, but that perception of matter and energy was quite clear and concrete for me. There were no longer any boundaries between solids and gases, between tree and sky, or between the wall of a house and the consciousness that perceived that wall.

Many years later, I realized that there was no way I could have seen my father sitting at my bedside in the hospital that night. He had come in very quietly. The room had been darkened because of the effects of light on my eyes. At the time my father entered I was deep in a coma, my eyes closed, my senses, as far as anyone knew, closed off from the world. Moreover, my father, years later, confided to me that he had never told anyone about the purpose for his visit. How, then, had I been able to know that he had gotten that call from the doctor, or that it was two a.m., or that he was alone in his grief because he had elected to protect my mother and other members of the family from the news that I might die?

After my complete recovery from the disease, I often relived the experience I'd had of moving through space and touching the *other side*. It was, and is, a vivid recollection, even to this day. But it was not until nearly twenty years later, while reading Kubler-Ross, that I found any real world confirmation for that experience. Kubler-Ross's patients had many times reported similar experiences. Kubler-Ross called it the near-death experience.

There are numerous explanations for the near-death experience. Some say it may be protective fantasy that the species has evolved as part of the death process, much like the self-anesthesia that occurs with serious physical injury. Others say that it is truly an experience of what it is like on the *other side*. I have no answers for this. What I do know is that the inner world experience I had about my father that morning in the hospital was accurate. I could trust the perceptions I had of why he was there and what was going on in his mind—even though we didn't communicate verbally, and even though I was unconscious at the time. It can be said that my knowledge of my father was such that I could have "mentally constructed" the image I had of him, stimulated by the subliminal awareness of his presence. So be it! The fact still remains that my inner world perceptions at that moment were accurate and trustworthy, and ultimately that is the only point I wish to make here.

The second experience that guided me toward trusting my inner world occurred in the early 1960s. I was in my mid-twenties at the time and like many others of my generation, was experimenting with mind-altering drugs. Under the guidance of a person who had studied how it was administered and how it was used by the Native Americans (himself a modern-day shaman), I took peyote on several occasions over a two or three year period.

With peyote, I saw how my inner world colored and gave shape to my outer world. Indeed, during long hallucinatory periods, I saw and spoke with people who had previously appeared only in my inner world, but now these people took on separate identities, including what appeared to be real physical bodies in the external world. It was as though I had projected my mental holograms outside myself. My shaman friend encouraged me to speak with these apparitions, which I did. As I spoke with them, sometimes aloud, sometimes only inwardly, I recognized that they had always been a part of me, that they had lived in my consciousness, appearing in my dreams and daydreams, for as long as I could remember. I also saw that they had a great deal to do with how I operated in the world; my interests, fears, likes and dislikes all related to my relationships with them.

When the peyote had worn off, I discussed what I had experienced with my shaman friend. He smiled and nodded, his face placid and maybe a little bemused, as though it was all common knowledge. I wanted explanations. If he had explanations, he wasn't about to give them. In the end he just looked me in the eye and said, "That's right." Annoyed at his glibness, I probed further. *What* was right? Was this the way everyone's inner world worked? "There is no inner and outer. It is all the same thing," he replied irritably. The subject was closed. The next thing I knew we were climbing into my car and driving across town to have breakfast at a Denny's restaurant near the freeway onramp.

Reflecting on the peyote experiences and my conversations with the people who lived in my consciousness, it seemed to me that I was, in my conscious life, like an emissary between inner and outer worlds. It was as though in my conscious life my task was to gather information, carry out experiments, and fulfill missions to satisfy the needs of the ethereal inner world.

Over the next two or three years, I took peyote perhaps a dozen or more times, sometimes alone, sometimes with my shaman friend, sometimes with others. Thanks to the hallucinogens, I could carry on long conversations with the entities of my inner world, question what purpose this or that inner guide served in my life. On one occasion I even had a showdown with a character who had played tricks on me and manipulated me over the past years. Even while all this was occurring, I knew the difference between these ethereal manifestations and the "real" people in my life. At no time was I fearful that I was in danger of losing my mind. This *work* seemed as natural and meaningful as anything I could imagine doing. Rather than fear or bewilderment, I finally experienced a great sense of relief, a feeling of "Aha! At last all the cards are on the table!"

■

THE HEALING PARADIGM

In the late 1960s, my interest in the exploration of the inner world became focused on healing. At first I did not understand the relationship between this interest and my interest in the inner journey. But over the months it became increasingly clear. I was attracted to healing because it seemed to offer a "proving ground" for testing the relationships between body and mind. Healing became the metaphor for discovering where the material self (the body) left off and where the consciousness (inner world) took over.

The key question for me was, and still is, to what extent is consciousness dependent on the physical self, and vice versa? I was attracted to situations where people seemed to be able to change the condition of their physical bodies by changing their attitude or their feelings or their inner perceptions about their lives.

Through a series of coincidences, I met Mike Samuels and his wife, Nancy, and through them I became acquainted with the Headlands Clinic, located in a small northern California coastal town, where Mike, an M.D., Dr. Irving Oyle, and other physicians and healers were exploring some of the same issues that interested me.

The Headlands Clinic is historically significant in that it grew from one of the first of a series of major ecological disasters—this one touched off when two oil tankers collided in the fog under the Golden Gate Bridge—that would alert the world community to the fact that what we had created with our minds over the past 200 years truly put our planet at risk. As never before in the modern world, the lesson was being driven home; we had to become caretakers of the Earth. Seeing the truth in this—manifest in our lives as a sticky oil slick that threatened a twenty mile strip of beautiful California coast, killing thousands of birds and other wildlife—we sought explanations to make sense of what was happening.

Almost immediately there was renewed interest in Native American thought. To many outsiders, the reasons for this interest were frequently misunderstood. Interest was stimulated not because people were seeking exotic lifestyles as a form of escape from the crises we were facing, but because in Native American thought they found a metaphor and a value system, a way of looking at our planet that helped define the needs that had become so apparent. For example, the Native Americans' vision of the planet as Mother Earth ceased to be a poetic nicety. Instead, it was quite apparent that this intimate and highly personal relationship with our planet was a literal truth that could no longer be neglected. By contrast, our view of the Earth as a storehouse of riches to be exploited for selfish interests had led the human race to their present status, where we were blindly destroying that which nourished and supported us.

As people were cleaning up the beaches following the collision of the tankers, someone photocopied the words of Chief Seattle, written in 1894, and circulated copies among the volunteers:

> *He treats his mother, the earth, and his brother, the sky, as things to be bought, plundered, sold like sheep or bright beads. His appetite will devour the earth and leave behind only a desert.*
>
> *This we know. The earth does not belong to man; man belongs to the earth. This we know. All things are connected like blood which unites one family. All things are connected.*
>
> *Whatever befalls the earth befalls the sons of the earth. Man did not weave the web of life; he is merely a strand in it. Whatever he does to the web, he does to himself.*

As though drawn to the site of the disaster by need, several serious students of Native American thought and several practicing shaman and medicine people (including Rolling Thunder, who would be the subject of Doug Boyd's book of that title) showed up at the Headland Clinic. Some led people in meditations, prayers and dances to give them strength to help heal Mother Earth from the deep wound the oil tankers had inflicted. And they began a dialogue on the need to spread the wisdom about our interdependence with the Earth. Years later, the importance of our recognizing this interdependence was echoed by Fritjof Capra, the speculative physicist who saw the link between our own consciousness and our planet, expressed both as a survival concern and a phenomenon that could be explained in the parallels between Taoist thought and modern physics.

After the beaches were cleaned up, Headlands transformed its identity from a first-aid station to a general medical clinic. Because of the life drama experienced by the people associated with Headlands, more traditional ways of viewing health opened up to broad new explorations and a new perspective on the healing philosophies of ancient cultures. Soon, physicians from all walks of life were coming to the clinic to find out more about the use of inner guides, Earth spirits, healing spirits, and the other ancient healing systems—acupuncture, hypnotherapy, herbology, massage—that were being explored.

Headlands excited my interest in the inner world and in my belief that this inner world plays a major role in every *conscious* act, no matter how rational or planned we may think we are being. The oil spill that inadvertantly gave birth to Headlands Clinic showed us all that health was much more than an individual issue; it was a broad global one. We could not have individual health without planetary health. And planetary health could only be produced through individual evolution, that is, by people like you and me developing what looked very much like a spiritual link with Mother Earth.

Healing was, as the Native Americans believed, the highest of all quests, because it depended on establishing understanding and a co-operative relationship with the life force itself. In their terms, such quests were religious in nature, being a person's search for understanding, for a way through the maze that is life. Healing ourselves or our planet is not, I learned, an exact science, but an art, and, at its best, a spiritual discipline that makes full use of what we know of the inner world.

In perceiving healing relationships as art or spiritual disciplines, we begin to see that the quality of the healer's relationship to his patient—be that patient one person or the planet—is determined by his mental attitudes and self-knowledge, which may hold at least as much power to cure as all the surgery or miracle drugs or herbs or medicine dances ever invented by the human race. That self-knowledge comes only by getting acquainted with the inner world.

■

A PERSONAL HEALING QUEST

Although I have always been intrigued by the inner world, and have felt that it was somehow my mission in life to explore it, the reasons why I should get to know it and what I was supposed to do with this knowledge have not always been clear to me. There have been times when I thought the best thing to do was to bury what I knew, to keep it a secret from the world—because in the places where I've lived and worked, and even in some of my most intimate relationships, the subject has been met with skepticism at best, if not outright hostility and distrust. In recent years, however, it has become clear to me that learning how to deal with this skepticism and resistance has been part of the lesson I am intended to learn. My knowledge, more recently, has allowed me to form a bridge between two worlds— the world of the technocrat and the world of the mystic.

As I have become increasingly outspoken about my knowledge, I notice that I have also become increasingly impatient with fuzzy explanations and applications of the inner world skills of the quasi-mystics. And it has become important to me to separate myself and my thinking from a popular movement that views all this as a kind of magic. It is not, in my view, magic. And to view it as such dilutes its power and its usefulness.

Because of my strong feelings about this, I was, in the beginning, reluctant to use my abilities as an *intuitive* or psychic. Using those skills in healing relationships to assist other people—which seems to be part of my calling —is not something to be taken lightly. I went through a personal crisis about this. And as might be suspected, the resolution of that crisis—its healing—came through the same channels that precipitated the crisis.

The crisis peaked about the time I was commissioned to do some writing for two healers, who would later become close friends of mine. In the process of experiencing the work of these people, I felt more than ever that I had a real contribution to make, and that my own stubbornness about offering my knowledge and abilities to others was nothing but a kind of reverse vanity. Whatever gifts I had were not, after all, mine to lay claim on; they fell into the realm of universal knowledge that no one person could justifiably "own."

Susan, my wife, encouraged me. She is a bodyworker and healer, and there were many times she asked me to assist her, to "read" a client who was having particular health problems. I did so reluctantly and at times felt pushed. But the quality of the work I did in this way should have been enough to convince me that I was on the right path. Still, I didn't feel ready. And I finally withdrew, deciding that I would keep my abilities and knowledge under wraps forever.

I not only avoided healing relationships where I might be called upon to use my intuitive abilities, but I turned to writing about business and computers so that I would not have to think very much about my inner world. But instead of feeling more comfortable with myself, I felt worse. The harder I tried to make a go of it in that world, the worse I felt. In time, I even lost sight of what I was trying to avoid. And then I had the following experience, which completely reversed my stand.

■

THE SHAMAN OF NEW ORLEANS

I was asked by a publisher with whom I was working to interview a "Dr. M" in Louisiana. Apparently, Dr. M. was combining shamanic tools of the American Indians with standard western medicine. Arrangements were made for me to fly to New Orleans, where I would be picked up at the airport and taken to the small clinic where this doctor worked.

From the beginning, nothing seemed to go right. The plane was delayed several hours owing to an electrical malfunction. We were grounded for repairs in Dallas. By the time we got into the New Orleans airport, I was irritated and exhausted, it was eleven o'clock at night, and there was no one to meet me. Finally, I heard my name being paged and eventually made contact with two men who said they had been sent by Dr. M.

The two men looked like farm laborers, both dressed in old jeans and flannel shirts. I guessed they were both in their late fifties or early sixties.

It was past midnight when we finally got to their car. I am not certain how it happened, but the next thing I knew I was sitting in the driver's seat of their battered old Chevy, clutching the steering wheel nervously as I raced through the night. We had left New Orleans and were driving on a high-crowned gravel road, bathed in the glow of my headlights, racing nervously along at a dizzying speed. I was more than a little frightened and wanted more than anything else to get to Dr. M's.

The territory through which we were driving was strange to me. It was a swampy area, and on either side of the narrow road that cut through the swamp were ditches, six to ten feet deep, posing a real danger were we to drive off the road. I was aware of a jungle of dark, primordial foliage beyond the ditches.

In the back seat my would-be escorts were sharing a fifth of whiskey, passing it back and forth between them as we raced through the darkness. The radio was blaring, tuned to a Mexican station playing Mariachi music.

I was drowsy and irritated, fighting to stay awake. One of the men in the back seat, speaking with an anachronistic Boston accent that he had begun to affect, was telling me that if I drove very fast I would have a better chance of staying awake. Adrenalin would keep me alert, he said. His companion laughed raucously when he said this.

Every time I dropped my speed below fifty-five or sixty miles per hour, my fellow passengers started screaming at me: "Drive faster! Faster! Faster!" I was certain they were totally insane, and motivated by the desire to escape their behavior by getting to Dr. M's as quickly as I could, I complied with their wishes.

In spite of my efforts to stay awake, my eyes fluttered closed. Even as I drifted off to sleep, with blackness and a sense of foreboding overtaking me, I was aware of the consequences, and I fought my way back to consciousness. The car had left the road, and was plunging down into the ditch!

I clutched the wheel in my hands and wrestled the car back up onto the road. While all this was happening, I was aware of my passengers laughing uproariously, thoroughly enjoying my plight—and apparently delighting in the danger.

Back on the road, I slowed down, but my passengers screamed at me to drive faster, their voices mingling with the blaring voices of the mariachi singers on the radio—until at last I did as I was told. At eighty miles per hour the road became a blur.

A sharp turn appeared before me. The man with the British accent, who sat directly behind me, reached forward and sprayed something in my face, from a bottle that resembled a windex sprayer, just as I started into the turn. Instantly, my eyes closed and I drifted toward sleep, aware of the car plunging downward into the ditch at eighty miles per hour.

I struggled back to consciousness, again to the uproarious laughter of my apparently insane passengers.

This same event was repeated many times over as we traveled for thirty miles or more through the swamp. After the second or third time it happened, I realized that as I fell asleep I immediately began to dream, and in the dream I was standing outside all of this, watching it dispassionately. I seemed to move outside my body, even outside the car. In fact, I seemed to be viewing what was happening from a vantage point about twelve feet behind and six or eight feet above the car, and I recall thinking of myself as having taken the body of a hawk. As a hawk, I looked through the metal roof of the car, as though I had x-ray vision. I saw myself slouched behind the steering wheel. I saw the two men in the back seat, passing a bottle back and forth, totally caught up in what appeared to be an intense philosophical discussion. The two passengers never showed the least indication of being concerned about their welfare, even when the car drifted off the road and headed down into the ditch. They did not, in any way, share my anxieties.

At last it occurred to me that no matter what the dangers seemed to be in my mind, I had been able every time to pull out and save us all at the very last moment. This came as a great revelation to me.

"What are you thinking?" the man with the Boston accent asked me, as though he was able to read my mind.

"I just realized that regardless of what happens, we are in no real danger," I replied. "No matter what happens to the car or to us, we are safe."

Someone reached forward with the sprayer and gave me another shot of mist right in the face. I was aware of dampness on my skin. And then my eyes clamped shut, and I fell into a deep sleep. I fought to regain consciousness, but as I did so, I experienced no sense of danger as I'd done before. I calmly awakened, steered back up onto the road and we continued on our way.

"You see," I said. "There's your proof. No matter what happens, it turns out all right."

The second man asked the first what I had said. The first man answered him in a language I didn't understand —it was neither English nor Spanish—and they both laughed wildly.

"He's learning," the second man said in a broken accent. I was aware then that he was a Mexican, probably a Mexican bracero. "By the time we arrive he will be a much wiser man," the bracero said.

The first man reached forward to spray me in the face again. This time, I grabbed the bottle from his hand and flung it to the floor near my feet.

"Enough of that," I said. "It's some kind of drug, isn't it? That's what's putting me to sleep. You guys are crazy. You could have gotten us killed."

This was met with peals of laughter. And then, my fellow passengers began talking excitedly between themselves in that foreign-sounding language that I didn't understand.

In spite of the fact that I had captured their windex bottle, I fell asleep several more times before we arrived at our destination. But even though the same thing happened each time—falling asleep, awakening to find the car diving down into the ditch, saving it at the last moment—I completely lost any sense of fear or danger. I was confident that we could not be hurt.

Our destination, as it turned out, was a tiny shack in the middle of the swamp. I pulled into a clearing in front of it and shut off the engine of the car. As we climbed out, I was seething with anger.

The man with the Boston accent asked me why I was so mad. He was obviously amused, playing with me.

I listed my complaints: I didn't like their drinking; I resented their urging me to drive faster and faster; their maniacal laughter as I struggled to save us all from certain death, time and time again, was totally inappropriate; and, finally, the little trick of spraying me in the face with that stuff that made me fall asleep could have gotten us all killed.

The bracero handed me the windex sprayer, which he had retrieved from the floor of the car. "You mean this little thing?" he said mockingly.

I grabbed it, unscrewed the top and smelled the contents. It smelled like ordinary water.

"*Agua*," the bracero said, laughing. "Just regular water, amigo." He stopped, and then in perfect English said, "Do you really think we are fools enough to play with fate that way? My friend, we would never tempt the gods this way." And then he laughed.

I poured the contents of the bottle onto the ground and tossed the empty container into the underbrush.

We went into the shack where the Mexican struck a match and lit a kerosene lamp. I got the impression it was his house. I lay down on a cot in one corner of the all-purpose room. The two others sat down in straight-backed chairs on either side of a kitchen table. I was feeling sick to my stomach.

My companions asked me what was wrong. I told them that I felt ill, that perhaps it was something I'd eaten that day.

"Then go puke," the Mexican said, pointing to a toilet surrounded by a thin curtain in the opposite corner of the room.

I knelt down in front of the toilet and vomited. I immediately began choking, and in the dim light saw something like a clear-colored, gelatinous mass, something like a jellyfish, protruding from my mouth. I retched reflexively, and at last it fell into the brackish water in the toilet bowl.

There was a bland taste in my mouth and the gelatinous stuff was sticking to my teeth and the back of my tongue.

I was aware, then, of the Mexican at my side. He patted me on the back consolingly, which calmed me.

"Drink this," he said. "It will help."

He handed me a shot glass that contained a clear liquid. I drank it down, and instantly my mouth and throat felt better. My stomach also felt good.

"What is that stuff?" I asked.

"It is bitter herbs," the Mexican said.

"How is he doing?" the man with the Boston accent asked behind us.

"He's fine. I think he's got it now. He's cleared it all out."

"That's great!" the other man said.

I turned away from the toilet and came back to the cot where I'd been resting when I first came in.

The man with the British accent grabbed my hand and shook it. "Congratulations," he said. "That's wonderful. Things will go much better for you from now on."

I did not know exactly what all this meant, but I knew I felt about as good—physically as well as mentally —as I had ever felt in my life.

■

Like the conference with Jung, Einstein, Chardin, and Poshaiankia, the above took place on the screen of my consciousness, except that the conference took place in a waking state as I sat in front of my computer, and the drive through the swamp was a dream, occurring while I was sound asleep. I remembered it in great detail and immediately wrote it down in a notebook I keep beside my bed. I tell the story for reasons that will become obvious in a moment.

Approximately a year before this dream, I had "read" one of my wife Susan's clients who was from the South and who had told me about a physician like Dr. M, who had once treated her. Like my doctor in the dream, hers also was from a town near New Orleans. This woman was having trouble with her neck and shoulder. As Susan worked on the woman, I had gotten a clear picture of her lying injured on a road, with a crowd of people gathered around her. There had been an accident. There was a lake nearby, and it seemed to me that it was in the mountains somewhere, a kind of resort area.

When Susan was done working with the woman, I told them what I had seen. The woman listened intently, then said, "I was never in an auto accident."

The woman thought for a moment, then added, "You know, my sister was in an accident. There was an auto accident in Switzerland, where she was traveling at the time. She was nearly killed. One of her injuries was a broken shoulder."

As we discussed this further, I learned that her sister and she were twins. They had been extremely close throughout their entire lives. As children, they had even shared a private language, known only to themselves. In adulthood, as was true with many twins, they always felt that they were in communication with one another, regardless of the miles that separated them. They even shared many of the same diseases and injuries! For example, both had recently had cancer surgeries involving the same areas of their bodies.

Later, in confirming the details of the accident with the woman's twin, we did find that it had taken place near a lake, and that she had lain in the road for nearly an hour before help came.

A few weeks after the work Susan and I did with the woman, she came to see us with her sister. During that meeting, the sisters came to the realization that they were maintaining their interdependence as twins through disease and injury and emotional conflict! They resolved to be more aware of this and to focus more attention on healthy and positive things to share.

My success with this reading, and the benefits the sisters gained from it, should have convinced me even then that I had something valuable to share in this way. Yet it didn't. I resisted the obvious. And the more I resisted it, the more crazy things felt to me.

The dream which I've recorded above is directly related to that event for me. The following is how I have interpreted its meaning:

The swamp through which I drove in the dream represents the unknown territory of the psychic world. In the dream, I was racing into it at a speed which I found dizzying. I like to go slowly, one careful step at a time. I was afraid that I would lose control, "fall asleep at the wheel," and crash.

Who were the men in the back seat? I think they both represented shamans and psychics to me, appearing as down-to-earth laborers, which gave the psychic theme a reality and *groundedness* and *maleness* that I needed for my own confirmation. The man with the British accent was, I believe, Alex, the inner guide who has been important in my life for many years. I had never seen him dressed as he was in the dream, but I am certain it was him. The second man's name, as it turns out, was Roy, and Roy is still with me, having become a trusted inner companion.

In the drive through the swamp, I was assured over and over again—not only by the experience itself, but by my companions—that the loss of control I feared in this "psychic swamp" was okay, that I was not "tempting fate," that I was not in danger no matter what I thought or felt. And finally, in my getting sick and vomiting at the shack in the swamp, I cleared my throat and *found my own voice.*

How did I come to these understandings of my dream? My process is very simple. I record the dream just as it occurred. Then I read the dream back to myself several times, often over a period of weeks or months, asking what its meaning might be in the same way I might ask the meaning of a well written story or poem. I look at the events taking place in the real world for me at that time, and I ask myself if anything there relates to the dream. The result is usually a merging of inner and outer realities, with answers coming like little revelations, a gut level response of "Aha! That's it!" whenever I strike on an interpretation that works for me.

As a direct result of this dream, I made the decision to write this book. I also made the decision to apply my skills and knowledge of the inner world whenever the need arises. I have begun to have more and more people coming to me for readings. I have been able to structure my reading work so that people can translate what I see into positive actions in their lives. Sometimes the resolutions they work out as a result of the readings are practical, such as a decision to change careers. At other times they are emotional, such as resolving a long-time conflict with a parent or sibling or mate. And sometimes they are purely physical, such as getting relief from chronic pain.

Now, as I write about the inner world, I realize that I have never felt better or more confident about anything I've written in my life. There is a profound sense of "coming home," of the material being truly mine, of my *finding my own voice*.

■

THE FOUNDATIONS OF MY WORK

When I was a small boy growing up in Michigan, I had an imaginary friend who I called Alex, who of course also appears in the above dream. Alex was like a trusted older brother, eight or ten years my senior and, I believed, infinitely wiser than I in the ways of the world.

When Alex and I were together, we talked. Walking down the street in the suburban neighborhood where I lived, we carried on lengthy inner dialogues, and, to me, Alex was as "real" as any other person in my life.

My parents were *tolerant* when I told them about Alex, though I am certain that had they understood how important he was in my daily life, they might have been more concerned. Where I grew up, the idea of "talking to yourself" was not considered to be healthy behavior. My parents' reaction, at worst, was to indulge me, treating my stories about my imaginary friend as "cute make-believes" that I would eventually outgrow.

If my parents indulged me, my peers were less than kind. After suffering through the jibes of my playmates about "the little man who wasn't there," I found that I was better off not mentioning him. I pushed my thoughts about Alex to the back of my mind, as though it was something not quite acceptable. And Alex's presence in my life, at least on a conscious level, became less and less important.

In my twenties, I became interested in C. G. Jung's writings, which gave me at least a hint of support and confirmation for my experiences with inner guides. Jung spoke of the *anima* and *animus,* figures that appear in our unconscious, and which seem to us to be autonomous—that is, spirit beings with personalities that are separate from our own.

Jung said that his theories about the anima and animus were "not a question of anything *metaphysical.*" Yet, he admitted that the spirits or inner guides could be "as rich and strange as the world itself," and that as we begin "making them conscious we convert them into bridges to the unconscious." For Jung, the anima and animus represented male and female functions or personal characteristics that, for highly individualized reasons, were important to the person's overall vision of life. He claimed that these spirits and their functions had been noted by people in "primitive" societies for centuries.

It is interesting to note that many years later, while reading the work of the Northern Cheyenne philosopher and medicine man Hyemeyohsts Storm, I came upon these words: "Within every man there is the Reflection of a Woman, and within every woman there is the Reflection of a Man. Within every man and woman there is also the Reflection of an Old Man, an Old Woman, a Little Boy, and a Little Girl."

As important as the functions or characteristics associated with the anima might be to us, we could not, or had not yet allowed ourselves to incorporate them into our personalities, according to Jung. This might be for negative reasons. For example, an anima might embody characteristics that we considered distasteful, and which we could not accept as part of our own personality. Or we might reject it for what others might view as positive reasons. For example, an anima could embody a sense of self-power that we could not imagine ourselves possessing because to do so would mean that we would have to give up the security of a dependency on a parent or other loved one. In order to have these characteristics in our lives without fully "owning" them, we invented these spirits of the unconscious so that we could have some of the benefits of these characteristics without fully incorporating them into our personality.

To maintain our separateness from these character-istics and, at the same time, experience a sense of completeness in our outer world, Jung postulated, we might seek relationships with real people who matched, or as closely as possible matched the anima that lived within our consciousness. There were dangers, however, in seeking the real world *double* of these spirits; people in the outer world could never quite fill the bill. They would be mere *stand-ins* who would leave us frustrated and bewildered. In addition, therapeutic work with people who attempted to do this, Jung found, revealed that the anima might defend its territory like a jealous lover, or an overprotective parent, acting hurt or angry whenever we approached a person in the real world who might replace them. In that case, our emotional involvement with the anima or animus might result in our acting to protect that inner guide.

Jung believed that we could transform these guides from being sources of conflict in our lives to becoming real helpers. We do that by speaking to the inner guide, asking questions of it such as why is it present in our lives. For example, Allen—a friend of mine who went through Jungian analysis—reported having difficulty maintaining lasting relationships with women. He desperately wanted a stable relationship, but whenever he became close to a woman he liked, he began to act in an offensive and "chauvinistic" manner which would drive her away. Though he intellectually understood what he was doing, and did not like himself when he was being chauvinistic, he could do nothing to stop himself.

In the course of his work with the Jungian therapist, Allen discovered that he had an inner guide who was a middle-aged woman called Alice.

47

Alice embodied all the human values that he had been taught were "feminine." Although he felt a need for these feminine qualities in his life, he was unable to allow himself to consider them as elements of his own personality because, according to his father's values, this would have made him a "sissy."

Allen eventually discovered that Alice was jealous of his relationships with the real women in his life, and it had been as a result of protecting Alice that he had manifested the chauvinistic behavior that drove away his prospective lovers.

Eventually, Allen started talking directly with Alice, treating her as if she was an actual person in his life. He told her that she must stop interfering with other relationships in his life. He went through a period of feeling guilty for doing this. But he realized that as an adult he had every right to determine who and what entered his consciousness. Soon after this, Allen did establish a successful relationship with a woman, and was eventually happily married.

Following his laying the law down to Alice, this anima eventually adopted a helpful role in Allen's life. He turned to her whenever he wanted guidance in emotional matters. It was, after all, the woman's job to take care of such matters—or so he had been led to believe by his parents. In time, Alice was transformed from being a source of conflict in his emotional relations to being a real helper.

One rather interesting aside is that after he was married, Allen became interested in cooking, and it soon became a deeply satisfying creative outlet—though it had been assigned to the woman's world in his father's eyes. When he was cooking, Allen said, he always had a strong sense of Alice's presence, as though she was helping him and enjoying his culinary creativity as much as he.

■

BEYOND ANIMA AND ANIMUS

Jung and other psychologists have noted that not all of the contents of the anima or animus are the products of the person's ego or personality. Often, the entities that Jung called anima/animus appear spontaneously in dreams, or through the use of *active imagination* (guided imagery or visualization), but in no way do these entities or their histories appear to be related to other issues that the person is dealing with, and so would appear quite separate from the person perceiving them. For example, "channeled" entities such as Seth, or Ramtha, whose wisdom and personal histories appear to be quite outside the everyday realms of the persons receiving their words, would have to be viewed as something other than anima/animus.

In his memoirs, Jung described a conversation he had with his own spirit guide, Philemon, which should help shed some light on this subject:

> *I observed clearly that it was he (Philemon) who spoke, not I. He said I treated thoughts as though I generated them myself, but in his view thoughts were like animals in the forest, or people in a room, or birds in the air, and added, 'If you should see people in a room, you would not think that you had made those*

> *people, or that you were responsible for them.' It was he who taught me psychic objectivity, the reality of the psyche...He confronted me in an objective manner, and I understood that there is something in me which can say things that I do not know and do not intend..."*

The mystery about the source of these entities remains, but we do know that there are many records of conversations with such beings, most of them highly beneficial, which in many cases continued for many years.

■

THE WORLD OF DOLL SPIRITS

While I, during my boyhood, had an imaginary playmate, I recall that the girls I knew during that time had favorite dolls that they treated and talked about as though they were real people. Doll tea parties were not unusual. Indeed, such practices were encouraged by the stories of many childrens' writers. This personification of dolls is not unlike the use of fetiches in the Zuni medicine societies.

In a workshop I once gave, one woman spoke of her teddy bear, a battered and worn, many times mended, stuffed toy which had originally belonged to her grandfather. She still had the teddy bear, and still thought of it whenever she was facing a major decision in her life. (She was the head of a large real estate brokerage.) Another woman spoke of a Barbie doll which she owned, and which she still kept in the bottom of her dresser. She could not allow herself to give it away. The odd thing was that this woman was far from being the Barbie doll type—if there is such a thing. Her Barbie was, she explained, very grownup and independent; she described the doll as her "model for the liberated woman. She always knew the right answers."

Men and boys also have dolls, but until very recently this was not as acceptable for males as it was for females. Males are more likely to attribute human qualities to a toy car or truck, and in late adolescence, when they get real cars, the same *persona* assigned the toy in childhood may be transferred to the car.

The important thing to note in all these personifications of inanimate objects is that they represent "real" personalities to the person who treats them thus. These personifications are created out of the stuff of the consciousness, and as such they are bridges to the inner world. The external object is not the most important factor here; what is important is that the person is creating that personality in their own mind, and the relationship they establish with that personality is significant for them. They may talk over their problems with that personality; they may go to it and receive emotional comfort. In short, they may get as much from this "imaginary being" as they get from some of the real people in their lives.

It is my experience, moreover, that the people who have guides of this kind in their lives do not use them as substitutes for real friendships. In fact, the opposite seems to be true. In discussing this with me, one man told me that he thought his imaginary playmate—in his case, a stuffed monkey that a favorite aunt had made for him for his third birthday—allowed him to enjoy his real friendships more fully since he did not feel the need to burden his friends with some of the deeply personal issues that he addressed to his toy monkey.

■

INNER GUIDES AS TEACHERS

In following Jung's model, I found that my task with at least some of the inner guides I encountered became one of accepting their importance in my inner life, and then allowing myself to learn from them, setting up the same kinds of sometimes skeptical, sometimes fully trusting relationships that I had with people in my outer world. And I found, indeed, that as I grew to know them, to recognize and accept their *human* strengths and weaknesses, my own personality took on their functions, just as it had done for the man in the above example with the guide called Alice. I could *own* the functions of character they represented.

In the 1970s, I happened upon the research of Elmer and Alyce Green, published in their book *Beyond Bio-feedback*. Their bio-feedback research, through the Menninger Foundation, made it clear that: "the unconscious mind did not distinguish between an imagined and a real experience." That which was *imagined* could have as dramatic affects on the body and the conscious mind as that which was experienced in the *real world through the senses*.

What bearing did this discovery have on inner guides? For me it was a great revelation; it indicated that in the final analysis it did not matter what the inner guides really were. The unconscious mind, which psychologists and neurophysiologists agree is the dominant force in our lives, experiences these persona just as it does any other "people" in our lives.

Given their potential influence on us, the first question that came to my mind was this: "How can I distinguish between an anima who may be mis-advising me, or giving me wrong information, in order to protect her own interests and one who has my welfare in mind?" How could I determine who could be trusted and who couldn't in this inner world? I concluded that no matter whether they were real or imagined, one had a responsibility to himself to weigh the value of whatever these beings brought to our lives. Sometimes they were right, sometimes they were wrong. Sometimes they were kind, sometimes cruel.

Whether they were real or not, one had to treat them as being, after all, "only human," just as capable of vanity and folly and error as the rest of us.

CHAPTER TWO:

Systems for Making Contact with Inner Guides

In 1969, Mike Samuels and I started talking about writing a popular medical book that would demystify medicine and introduce people to the idea of broadening their visions of health. One morning when I arrived at Mike's house for a brainstorming session, he told me about a conversation he had recently had with his spirit guide, Braxius. I had never heard about Braxius before, but Mike described him as a "giant, jeweled praying mantis." Though I found it a bizarre if not offputting image, the ideas Braxius had discussed with Mike were indeed quite remarkable.

We began discussing a process Mike had learned for using guided imagery to get a spirit guide. I was deeply interested in this because until then, I'd never heard of any systematic way to do this. My own guides had always appeared spontaneously, and there didn't seem to be a way to call them at will.

That afternoon, sitting on the deck that overlooked

his orchard, Mike took me through the guided imagery program that he had learned at the Headlands Clinic. He read me instructions to relax my body and let go of my ego concerns. As I relaxed, I had the sensation of drifting weightlessly and comfortably into space, not unlike the experiences I'd had traveling in my inner world when I fell into a coma as a teenager sick with high fever.

Part of my mind felt as though it could be anywhere and that I could take any form I wished. The experience was intense, and in the beginning I was nervous about doing it. But the relaxation portion of the exercise made me very comfortable, almost blissful, and at last I became quite at ease with the process.

As I gazed out over limitless space, I had a clear vision of a Tudor mansion. It stood at the edge of a forest, surrounded by formal gardens. I saw a miniature version of myself standing on the lawn in front of this mansion. The whole scene was like looking at a tiny, highly realistic architectural model, except that it seemed real to me. The "me" on the lawn turned, faced me on the deck, and invited me to join him.

After I gave myself permission to do this, I had the sense of merging with the miniature me. But, as this occurred, my perspective changed, and the world appeared as its normal size. I became aware that although the mansion itself was hundreds of years old, I was in modern times; I was aware of the sound of automobile traffic on a highway some distance away.

I opened the door of the house and walked inside, passing along a wide corridor and then up a long flight of stone stairs. I came to a door, opened it, and went inside.

Inside the room I met a middle-aged woman with very close-cropped, salt and pepper hair, a round friendly face, and myopic eyes that were nearly hidden by the thick, milky lenses of her eyeglasses. She was short, stout, and wore a white lab coat.

She introduced herself as Hilda. She was a scientist and whe told me that she was conducting research on psychic healing. She told me that she believed psychic healing was a form of bio-feedback training, and that a healer was able to promote a cure because the sick person's unconscious mind received a subtle message to change blood flow or redirect glandular functions, which themselves were the actual mechanism responsible for the healing, all of which was under our control through hypnotic suggestion. Hilda said that the placebo theory, known to medical science for over a hundred years, was a prime example of this. She said that her theories did not explain all such healings, but she had proof that she was right in a great many cases.

I asked many questions, and Hilda provided answers that I felt were quite rational. In the course of our conversation, she told me that I should not always think of myself as primarily a writer, because I had a capacity to see beyond words, and that it was important for me eventually to use my writing to show others how to develop this important skill.

In the room where I met Hilda, there was a *dark place.* By this I don't mean to imply anything forbidding. Rather, it was like a black hole in space, where nothing could be seen. When I looked more closely, however, I saw a tunnel reaching into infinity, in some ways reminding me of my near-death experiences. It was a little like looking into the eye of a tornado, but it was not, as I say, threatening in any way. Hilda explained to me that through this tunnel we could travel to any time or place that we wished.

She asked me if I would like to try this now, since there was something she wanted me to see. I agreed to do so. We then moved into this space. I felt a sensation of falling, twisting and spinning weightlessly through space. Ordinarily I would have gotten dizzy under such circumstances. This time I didn't. The twisting sensations stopped, and I found myself standing with Hilda in a jungle clearing, surrounded by a dense undergrowth of lush ferns.

Hilda said she wanted me to meet Utbanga, a healer whom she'd been studying. I agreed to this meeting, and she led me forward into another clearing, where I saw Utbanga. He was a black man, his face and chest painted with streaks of yellow or orange stain, dressed only in a loincloth. He was dancing around a shriveled old man who sat crosslegged on the ground with his head bowed, his hands folded with resignation in his lap.

I asked Hilda if Utbanga was healing this man. Hilda said no. The old man was dying, and Utbanga was helping him in his passage from life to death. She explained that Utbanga's movements guided the energy within the cells of the old man's body as he moved in what Utbanga called "the rhythm of the leaves." Hilda told me that she had seen Utbanga apply similar techniques when healing sick people, and, that most of the time, he was successful in bringing about a cure.

Hilda and I watched for a while, then entered the dark space again and returned to the room where I'd met her. Back in the clinical atmosphere of the room, she told me that she had been observing Utbanga and a number of other healers for many years. Utbanga, she said, communicated only non-verbally, through dance and movement. She compared this language to the hula dance of

Hawaii, though the specific expressive movements were quite different. She had learned to interpret what he said and had translated his healing dances to verbal descriptions that she would gladly share with me.

After quite a long visit, Hilda and I exchanged good-byes, and after leaving the room I returned immediately to my every day consciousness. Leaving my inner world, I found myself sitting in a deck chair on Dr. Samuels' porch. I told Mike about what I'd experienced, and for an hour or more we discussed the ideas I'd brought back from my inner adventure.

As I was telling Mike about the house where all this had taken place, I remembered that I'd seen that same house before. The first time I'd seen it was when I took part in a peyote research project in San Francisco. In both that peyote vision and in the inner guide experience I'd just had, the house had seemed ancient, and when I entered it, I had the same experience one usually has upon entering a house with a long history. There was a sense of being connected to the past. I am certain I have never seen this house in real life, yet it was clearly familiar to me when I met Hilda there.

Nearly fifteen years have passed since I met Hilda and Utbanga, and looking back over the notes I recorded then, I realize that both of these inner guides have helped me in the years between then and now. One of the most significant things for me, one that confirms my belief in the importance of such experiences—whether "real" or not, by any scientific measure—is that I have truly learned, as Hilda predicted, to "see beyond words," to catch glimpses of the truth that lies quite outside our verbal capacities or our capacity for reason.

The experience I had, of Hilda taking me to see Utbanga, is an event to which I have returned again and again through the years, whenever I needed a clear model for what is popularly known as "psychic" phenomena. Hilda's scientific skepticism has both inspired me to seek concrete explanations for such phenomena and supported me in learning to trust my own experiences and abilities in this realm.

What's more, I believe that the structured system for making contact with an inner guide, which Mike Samuels showed me that day, is perhaps one of the easiest methods for getting your own inner guides. Because it is both a dependable and safe method, I include a version of it in the back of this book.

■

SUCCESS WITH DIRECTED PROGRAMS FOR MAKING CONTACT WITH INNER GUIDES

At about the same time that Mike and I started working with inner guides, we settled on a title for the book we would do together. We named it *The Well Body Book,* and upon its completion, a year later, it became a highly respected and loved basic text for the self-help health movement, eventually to be published in five languages and distributed worldwide.

I mention this because while writing that book, Mike and I turned time and again to our inner guides. At one point, there was a long poem or song that was dictated to me by an American Indian shaman I met through the inner guide I called Hilda. Though that poem was never published, and has since been lost, it provided me with a very solid philosophy of medicine and healing that would be an important influence in my life forever after.

Because inner guides were so important to Mike and I, we decided that we would like to write a book about them. That was in 1972, soon after completing *The Well Body Book*. We called the new book *Spirit Guides: Access To Inner Worlds*. It was channeled to us through a guide called "Kishah." As we said in the introduction of that book, the experience of writing through Kishah was like having our "voices merge to create a third voice that had an identity all its own."

Spirit Guides was a tiny book, a scant 50 pages in length, that provided basic information about inner guides. Judging by the mail we got and the feedback we received from people in workshops who used it, the book was instrumental in encouraging people all over the country in making use of inner guides in their lives. Indeed, we received praise from a number of physicians, including a long letter from a Jungian analyst who told how the book described "some successful approaches toward experiencing the helpful resources which are present in those events of fantasy, daydreams, hunches, intuition, and feeling which we call our inner life."

In the years since writing that little book, I have learned a great deal more about the use of inner guides. My expanded work on the use of guides, as well as Zuni fetiches, healing circles, dreams, and visions carried me quite beyond what we had been able to accomplish in that first book on spirit guides.

The directed program upon which that book was based continues, I believe, to be an excellent place to enter your inner world. It provides structure and security, so essential for tapping into one's inner resources. And once a person establishes this kind of *grounding,* the directed program clearly provides the foundation for going much further.

■

PRELIMINARY INSTRUCTIONS FOR MEETING INNER GUIDES

The exercise I present here begins with relaxation. In a deeply relaxed state, your mind slows, and the visual cortex of your brain becomes more receptive and more active. It is here, in the visual cortex, that the action of the inner guide will first take place.

Much has been made, in recent years, of the importance of deep relaxation for exercises such as this. It is often taught as "meditation," and some meditation teachers make far too much fuss about it, giving the process a mystical connotation that I believe only confuses many people.

Everyone meditates. It is a human process that is as normal as eating or sleeping, a fact that was made quite clear in the work of Elmer and Alyce Green. Exercises are intended not to teach the basic skill so much as to teach how to do it at will.

However we meditate, be it in a disciplined way or by chance, our brainwaves are altered; we grow relaxed, so relaxed that we let go of the tensions and worries of the day and soon our minds go blank or nearly blank. In this state, we enjoy the feeling of having nothing to think about or act upon. For a moment we truly cut ourselves off from the cares of the world.

This deeply relaxed state is easily achieved with the following exercise, though it may take repeated practice (from three to six or more tries) before you feel you can achieve the deep state of relaxation at will.

■

FOR NEWCOMERS ONLY If you have never done a deep relaxation or meditation exercise before, the scenario will probably go something like this: You'll scan the written exercise, which will seem simple enough, almost too simple to be taken seriously. Then you'll decide to give it a try. You get all the way down to the middle section of the exercise with no trouble.

As you begin to relax, something comes to mind that simply must get done before you go on. Or, you begin going over events of the day. Or you begin to worry about something that at that moment you can't possibly do anything about anyway. And everything that comes to mind *really is important*. These are concerns that you ordinarily act upon in an automatic way, and which are integral to your life. It is important to remember this, and to remember that when beginning meditation, all the issues that are normally important in your life do become very pressing. The real challenge of meditation is in learning how you handle yourself in the next few moments.

Let yourself fully acknowledge the thoughts and feelings running through your mind. But tell yourself firmly, "I do not have to act on any of these issues right now. It is perfectly all right to take ten or fifteen minutes for relaxing. I can take time out from these concerns."

The issues, like spoiled children, may continue to try to capture your attention. You may resist their promptings, gritting your teeth, determined not to be drawn in. But if you do that you tense up, and something very peculiar happens. The issues escalate in their efforts to get your attention. What do you do now?

Stop and make a conscious decision. Ask yourself, Should I stop relaxing, get up and do what I feel I must do, or should I let it go? If you really feel you need to take care of something, do it. Don't make any bones about it. You can come back to relax after you have done what you must do. If there isn't time to come back to your relaxation exercise, put off the exercise for another day. This is not something that needs to be accomplished in a single sitting, or several sittings. Your decision to stop your meditation and do something else is as important to the process of learning deep relaxation as is a fifteen minute session with no interruptions.

■

FINAL TIPS ON DOING THIS EXERCISE

For best results, you may wish to do this exercise with a friend, having them read it to you as you follow the directions to relax. You might also wish to make a cassette tape of it on your recorder and play it back to yourself. If you do this, read the exercise into the recorder in a monotone. Read slowly enough so that you can complete each step of the exercise before going onto the next one.

Commercially produced relaxation tapes are also available in most book stores. These are often very effective, containing quiet background music to help you maintain a relaxed state for several minutes. Be sure, however, to choose one you enjoy. Because many of the commercial tapes do have music, and because people's tastes in music are so individualized, you may have to try a couple different tapes before you find one that works for you.

■

**THE
RELAXATION
EXERCISE**

Make a conscious decision to take five or ten minutes to relax. Give yourself permission to use your time in this way. Choose a time of day and a place to work where you will be free of distractions.

- Sit in an alert, upright position, your hands laying gently, palms open, on the tops of your legs.

- Let your shoulders be loose and relaxed.

- Relax your toes and let the entire soles of your feet make contact with the floor.

- Loosen any tight-fitting clothing.

- Open your mouth and yawn, or pretend you are yawning.

- Let the areas around your eyes be relaxed. Let your forehead be loose. Let the area around your nose and mouth be relaxed.

- If ideas or feelings urge you to think or act at this time, pretend they are a ringing telephone in another room.

You may observe the sound of the "ringing," but don't feel that you must answer. Simply focus your attention on the quality of the bell's sound and remind yourself that truly important thoughts or feelings will return, if you wish them to, after you have finished relaxing.

- Take a deep breath. Hold it for a moment. Slowly exhale through your nose.

Be aware of your chest relaxing.

- Take a deep breath. Hold it for a moment. Slowly exhale through your nose.

Be aware of your shoulders relaxing.

- Take a deep breath. Hold it for a moment. Slowly exhale through your nose.

Be aware of your abdomen relaxing.

- Take a deep breath. Hold it for a moment. Slowly exhale through your nose.

Be aware of your back and buttocks relaxing.

- Take a deep breath. Hold it for a moment. Slowly exhale through your nose.

Be aware of your legs relaxing.

- Take a deep breath. Hold it for a moment. Slowly exhale through your nose. Feel the bottom of your feet where they make contact with the floor.

Be aware of your feet relaxing.

- Now allow your breathing to return to normal. Enjoy this relaxed state.

- Just allow yourself to be in this relaxed state for a moment before you go on.

■

THE EXERCISE FOR MEETING YOUR GUIDE

While in a deeply relaxed state, do the following to receive your inner guide:

Imagine that you are out for a walk.

You may be walking in a city. Or in a small village. Or in a woods. Or alongside a stream. Or near a lake or other large body of water. You may be in the mountains or by the ocean.

You feel safe. You feel confident. You feel comfortable.

For a moment, just enjoy your walk.

You now approach a structure: it may be a small house, a large building, a rustic structure, a modern one. Stop for a moment and simply look at this structure.

Notice its size and style. Notice the area around it—other houses, open fields, and so on.

You now go up to the structure. You are standing at its entrance. You knock on the door or in some other way announce your presence.

You hear a voice in your mind, or you get some sort of signal to enter and go inside. You do this, feeling confident, safe, and comfortable.

67

Step inside. Close the door behind you.

Look around you. Take note of what you see: the color of the walls and floors; whether the rooms are bright or dark; the furnishings you see; any knick-knacks that come to your attention.

Somewhere in this house you will meet your guide. This meeting may occur in the room where you are now standing. It may occur somewhere else. You will know exactly where you should be for this meeting. Go to that place now.

Imagine that you are now sitting down in the room where the meeting will take place. You are facing a special door. It is a sliding door that will open from the bottom up.

Your guide is now standing behind the door, waiting to meet you.

The door slides up a foot or so, then stops.

You see your guide's feet. Take your time, now. Note what the guide is wearing: shoes and socks? what colors and styles? or is the guide barefoot?

The door slides open a little more until you are able to see everything up to their belt-line. Note what they are wearing. You may also see their hands at this time, if they are standing with their hands at their sides. Note any jewelry they might be wearing.

The door now slides up as far as their neck. Again, note their clothes, if any, their posture, their size. Note any unusual personal items—a necktie or kerchief, pens or other items in their pockets.

Now the door fully opens, and you see your guide's face for the first time. Take as close a look as you like.

Look at their hair. Look at their forehead. Look at their eyes. Look at their mouth and chin. Look at their ears. Look at their neck.

It is time to greet your guide. In your mind, or out loud if you wish, say "Hello, my name is _____. I understand that you are my inner guide. I'd like to know your name."

Your guide steps forward now and greets you. You may have a sense of them shaking your hand, or hugging you, or kissing you.

If you do not get a response right away, wait until you do get a response. This may come as a voice, clear and distinct, like someone talking in the room where you are sitting; or it may come as a name that suddenly pops into your mind.

Imagine, now, that you and your inner guide sit down together and begin conversing. Talk on any subject, but in the first meeting limit yourself to an exchange of only a few minutes.

When you feel like stopping, simply tell your inner guide that you wish to do so. Tell them that you are glad you met them and that you will come back to be with them, and converse with them another time. Shake hands, or in some other way bring a cordial closure to the meeting.

Now imagine yourself leaving the room where you met. Go to the front door of the building where you met and go outside.

When you are ready, take a deep breath. Open your eyes if they were closed. Yawn. Stretch. Slowly get up and walk around.

■

AFTER YOU HAVE MET YOUR INNER GUIDE

After meeting your inner guide, give some thought to the meeting. Did it go as you wished? Did this guide seem to be someone you would like to meet and talk with in the future? If not, recognize at this point that you need not see them again. You can go back at a later date, do the exercise again, and get another guide.

If you are not certain you want to keep your guide, give yourself some time to think about it. There is no rush. And always remember; where your inner world is concerned you are the master. You may find things that surprise you, but you can take control at any time you wish.

If you didn't get an inner guide your first time around, don't worry. You can try again. Or, your guide may appear quite unexpectedly to you in the next day or two. The guide may even appear in a dream.

Occasionally, people may resist letting go of the control they usually enjoy in the "real" world in order to enter this inner world where nothing can be confirmed through the senses. C.G. Jung reports that his first efforts to make contact with his inner world were not without misgivings. At the time of his first experiments there was little, if any, literature available on the subject. He did not know if he could enter his inner world without "becoming a prey of the fantasies," and only after many years of exploring this inner world—both his own and his patients'—was he convinced that it was a safe territory for him to enter. The following is his description of the first experience he had upon entering that world:

> *It was during Advent of the year 1913— December 12, to be exact—that I resolved upon the decisive step. I was sitting at my desk once more, thinking over my fears. Then I let myself drop. Suddenly it was as though the ground literally gave way beneath my feet, and I plunged down into dark depths. I could not fend off a feeling of panic. But then, abruptly, at not too great a depth, I landed on my feet in a soft, sticky mass. I felt great relief, although I was in complete darkness. After a while my eyes grew accustomed to the gloom, which was rather like a deep twilight. Before me was the entrance to a dark cave, in which stood a dwarf with a leathery skin, as if he were mummified.*

Over the years, Jung entered this territory time and time again, and for nearly a decade explored and got to know the various figures he met there. He reports that he learned much from his journeys, especially from the inner guide he would call Philemon. Still, he was puzzled about the source of the information he received from Philemon, and what purpose that guide's personage served in his life.

This question was not answered for Jung until more than fifteen years after his first inner world experiments, when he was visited by an Indian friend of Ghandi's. The two men spoke about the education of Indian holy men. The Indian told Jung that his own guru was Shankaracharya, who had been dead for centuries. Jung reports the following dialogue in his memoirs:

"Then you are referring to a spirit?" I asked.

"Of course it was his spirit," the Indian replied. "There are ghostly gurus too. Most people have living gurus. But there are always some who have a spirit for a teacher."

It was then that Jung accepted his inner guide, Philemon, as his own "guru," a man whose wisdom, Jung felt, far surpassed his own. Jung reported:

> *This information was both illuminating and reassuring to me. Evidently, then, I had not plummeted right out of the human world, but had only experienced the sort of thing that could happen to others who made similar efforts.*

Most of the time people are happy with the guides they get. Let's assume that you are, too. In the days ahead, take every chance you can find to think about your guide, just as you might do after meeting a new friend. In the process of doing this, their presence may become quite vivid for you. I don't mean that you will see them appear in the chair across the table or beside you as you stand in line at the supermarket. But you may feel their presence in much the way you do when thinking about a close friend. Take advantage of this moment to share any thoughts you might be having with your guide. You needn't talk aloud to them. Doing it in your mind is just fine.

Conversations with your guide need not always be on serious issues. You may pass the time of day with them. You may even share stories or jokes. It is not at all unusual to build up trust in your guide slowly, making small talk, getting to know them one step at a time, before entrusting this new relationship with a problem that is important to you.

■

GUIDES WHO APPEAR IN DREAMS

In the preceding pages, I have described how you might get an inner guide through the guided imagery exercise for that purpose. But guides may also appear spontaneously in dreams. The following is one of the best examples I have ever encountered of an inner guide appearing in a dream.

A number of years ago a friend, Tom Bailey, was going through a career crisis, and partly as a result of the pressure this caused in his marriage, he and his wife had separated. Tom came to me and asked if I thought he might benefit from working with an inner guide. I said I wasn't sure but there would be no harm in giving it a try.

I explained to Tom how he could use inner guides, and what precautions he should take in accepting advice from them in times of crisis. We then went through the entire exercise for making contact with a guide, but nothing happened. He did not make contact with a guide. It seemed to me that he was too preoccupied with his troubles to free himself of the tension he was feeling to focus much attention on the exercise.

About a week after our meeting, he called me on the phone to thank me for my help. He told me that a few nights after our meeting he had a dream. He confessed that he rarely remembered his dreams, but on this occasion he did. He dreamt that he was walking down the street at night (he lived in New York at the time) when he heard footsteps behind him. He grew anxious, afraid that he was being followed by someone who meant him harm.

He quickened his step, and as he did so, a voice called out to him. He thought the voice sounded friendly, so he stopped and turned. Out of the shadows there emerged a figure of a man, about his own age, dressed in what Tom described as "antique" clothes, probably something from the Colonial American period. My friend asked what this person wanted, and the person replied that he had come to help him through his present crisis.

My friend said that he awoke almost immediately, realizing that this was his inner guide. Still in a somnolent state, he sat up in bed and in his mind asked this person many questions. He told me that the dialogue he carried on with the guide was helpful, and the next day he began to act on some of the ideas that had come up in that talk. The inner guide was there whenever my friend needed him after that, though as far as he could recall, the guide never again appeared in a dream.

■

INNER GUIDES WITH A PRACTICAL SIDE

I think that it is important to remember that the inner guides aren't there just to guide us through emotional or spiritual crises. Short of scrubbing floors and changing the oil in your car, their help can be as mundane as you wish.

My friend Mike Samuels once asked me to take a

look at his car, which wouldn't start. There had been a time when I was a fairly good mechanic, but that was before they put computer operated fuel injection systems under the hood. This new technology is a complete mystery to me, so I told Mike I wouldn't even attempt to diagnose what was wrong. Jokingly, he said, why don't you do a psychic diagnosis? And I, in jest, said I'd give it a try. I asked Alex what was wrong with Mike's car. He said there was a flexible hose under the fuel injection system that had come loose. All that needed to be done was to reconnect it.

Mike lifted the hood of his car and looked in. Sure enough, there was the flexible tube hanging loose, just as my guide had described it. Mike put it back in place and the car started instantly. One can easily chalk this up to coincidence, but my attitude toward it is quite pragmatic; nothing is wasted by asking your inner guides for advice on any subject—especially when it looks like you might otherwise have to get your hands dirty.

■

ARE INNER GUIDES INFALLIBLE?

Like people with physical bodies, the inner guides can provide knowledge, comfort, counsel—in short, nearly all the qualities that we seek in our every day human relations. And just as in other relationships, the guides can be sources of conflict, frustration, and anger.

The same things are true of inner guides as are true of the people in our outer worlds. The illusions they are capable of weaving are no different than the illusions we weave for ourselves, or which we allow those we love to weave with us. We must see the inner guides as being just as fallible as other humans in our lives. I am here reminded of Sheldon Kopp's warning to all of us who travel a deliberate path of self-realization:

> *God tugs at the pilgrim's sleeve telling him to remember that he is only human. Each man is capable of warmth, of loving, of understanding, of extending himself, of being transparent and vulnerable to another. At the same time, and perhaps in the same proportion, he is capable of evil, sham, fraud, and destructiveness, of closing out the other and wantonly using him.*

Because our relationships with our inner guides do affect the conscious as well as unconscious minds, it seemed to me important to love them and to confront them with both gentleness and courage when we think it necessary, and to make certain that we can live at peace with them, or if not complete peace that we could at least hold our own with them, just as we must do with our most important business associates, our most intimate friendships, and with members of our own families.

CHAPTER THREE:

Oracular Dreams & Guiding Visions

There have been numerous examples of famous people in science, literature, and the arts who have reported visions, dreams, or conversations with inner guides that led to their solution of creative problems. The most famous, perhaps, is the story of Kekule, the 19th century chemist who discovered the structure of the carbon molecule. Kekule reported to the scientific community of his day that he had been working in his laboratory long hours when he sat down in front of his open fire and fell into a "dozing state." In this state, he suddenly thought he saw the figure of a snake with its tail in its mouth. This figure seemed very important to him, and an instant later he realized that it was his model for the closed ring, the molecular structure of carbon, a discovery that revolutionized the science of chemistry.

Another famous example involves the invention of the modern sewing machine. Its inventor, Elias Howe, dozed off at his workbench one day and dreamed of a spear with an eye in its tip. When he awoke, he realized that this was a perfect solution to a problem which he had been having with his invention; instead of having the thread come from the tail of the sewing needle, he would have the thread come from the head!

Jung himself had a series of dreams and visions, originally self-published as the *Septum Sermones,* which he said were the inspiration for his entire life works. Reflecting on the *Septum Sermones* in the last decade of his life, Jung said:

> *All my works, all my creative activity, has come from those initial fantasies and dreams which began in 1912, almost fifty years ago. Everything that I accomplished in later life was already contained in them, although at first only in the form of emotions and images.*

Having read this far in this book, you will have a good understanding of inner guides, how to meet them, and how to make use of them in your life. But what about dreams and visions? Medical research proves that everyone has dreams and visions, but not everyone is aware of them.

Ouspensky believed that we have dreams all the time,

> *from the moment we fall asleep to the moment we awake, but remember only the dreams near awakening. And still later I realized that we have dreams continuously, both in sleep and in a waking state...Dreams never stop. We don't notice them in our waking state amidst the continuous flow of visual, auditory and other sensations, for the*

same reason we don't see stars in the light of the sun. But just as we can see the stars from the bottom of a deep well, so we can see the dreams that go on in us if, even for a short time, we isolate ourselves...and achieve consciousness without thought.

So the task of learning how to work with our dreams is less a matter of "getting" dreams and visions as it is a matter of *getting in touch* with them, recalling them, and learning what to do with them. Why are we not more aware of our dreams?

The fact that we don't make better use of our dreams and visions is not, I think, a matter of having or lacking special intuitive or psychic abilities, but more a matter of simply not taking the time to view, or "read," our visions and dreams. Our own *busy-ness* robs us of the great knowledge, as well as the great pleasures we might find there. When one is awakened every morning by the alarm clock, signaling the leap from bed and the dash off to work, there really isn't time to contemplate the dreams that may be lingering in consciousness, often guiding us toward the goals we cherish in our lives. And when we sit in front of the television set in the evening bombarded by an endless stream of exciting visual imagery and sound, there simply isn't room in our visual cortices for anything more.

What can we expect from our dreams and visions? The following story should help to answer that.

■

A DEATH IN THE FAMILY Undoubtedly one of the most dramatic uses of guiding dreams, and one that confirmed my belief that they contained genuinely useful information, came for me upon hearing that my father was dying. Dad was nearly eighty years old at the time and had lived a full and, I believe, satisfying life. He was far better prepared for his death than I or any of my other family members were.

I had no idea how to deal with his death. I got the news of his illness over the phone, from 3,000 miles away, and immediately after that call I went to my office to make arrangements to fly back to Michigan to be with him in his last hours. As I sat in my room, I remembered that I had written down a dream I'd had of his death nearly two years before. Having done dream work for nearly twenty years, I had a great number of journals to go through, but I was finally able to find the dream of my father's death and study what it said.

In the dream, my father was lying in a hospital room. It was winter. There were two windows, one pointing east, one pointing north, and, looking to the east, I saw a huge harbor. There was a door leading from the north wall of this building down some wooden steps to a row of docks. In the dream, my father died and I saw his spirit leave his body. I then led his spirit—which still held the shape of his body—to a strange looking boat, whose pilot, a man dressed like a fisherman and approximately my father's age, stood on the deck waiting for him.

My father and the boatman greeted each other in a

friendly way. My father was a bit nervous, but not frightened. He seemed to be anticipating the meeting with a certain amount of excitement. The boatman and he shook hands, and then the two of them admired the boat, which had beautifully finished wooden decks. My father, having been a furniture manufacturer, had an eye for fine finishes.

At last the boatman told my father that it was time to go. Dad turned to me and to my surprise asked my permission to leave, which I gave him. He then went over a list he had of every family member, asking for confirmation that they were all doing all right. I reassured him that everyone was doing well, and that I was certain they would all give him permission to leave us. He then asked me to say goodbye to them for him, and I promised him that I would. Then he and I embraced, kissed, and he got into the boat. The dream ended with my standing on the dock watching the boat disappear out over the horizon.

I read the dream and wept. Then I thought about Alex, and in an instant he was there. When I told him about my father dying he said very quietly that I should go and be with him, and that I should be his *guide*. I was appalled by the suggestion. I argued with Alex that I knew nothing about such things, that I had never been with anyone dying and wouldn't know how to handle it.

Alex told me not to worry, that it would be difficult, but that I would get help along the way and the whole thing would go quite smoothly. In a rather humorous way, as though satirizing himself by making his voice sound very mysterious, he said, "The first person who will help you will be an older woman. Listen to everything she tells you. It will be extremely important to you." I did not take this statement seriously at first. In

83

fact, I was put off by it, thinking that Alex was being insensitive by clowning around at a very serious moment.

A few hours later, I went down to the travel agency to pick up my airplane ticket. On the way out, I literally bumped into an older woman. At first I didn't recognize her, but as I excused myself and stepped back, she introduced herself. She was a real estate saleswoman who had sold my wife and I our house several years before.

The woman asked where I was going. I replied that my father was dying and I was going back to the mid-west to be with him. She looked directly at me and—so help me—she said, "You must come to my office and talk to me right now. I have something very important to tell you." Being from Southern Italy, she spoke with a thick accent, the kind that often characterizes psychics and other mysterious people in grade B movies. I wondered if Alex's clowning, an hour before, had actually been intended to prepare me for this. I remember thinking that if this character had been in a movie I would have walked out of the theater.

Her office was a few doors from the travel agency, and we went there immediately. I sat down, and she told me how she had sat with her father when he died. It turned out her father died from exactly the same disease that my father was suffering. She gave me a huge amount of information about the disease and what would happen, how he would become extremely agitated and restless, and how he would hallucinate, and how I might comfort him. She also said that for her the experience of sitting with her father in his death had been a "great privilege," as "wondrous as the birth of her children," and that even though she deeply mourned his loss, being present with him in his death had enriched her life.

On the airplane to Detroit, I thanked Alex for encouraging me to listen to the older woman, to trust that the kind of help I needed would come. Alex told me to have faith that I would continue to get whatever help I needed, and to look upon the dream as a guide dream, a map of what I could do.

My brothers met me at the airport in Detroit, and that evening I went to the hospital. The man I saw in the bed bore only a vague resemblance to the mental image that I had of my father. His lips were parched and bleeding, and he was badly dehydrated despite an IV in his arm, feeding fluids into his failing body.

Dad was happy to see me. He asked about my trip from California, and asked about my sons. We made small talk, and from time to time he dozed off. In the beginning, he was peaceful and outgoing, though his strength was obviously failing. But as that day passed, then another and another, his mood changed. He became agitated and impatient with the medical staff, didn't want them in his room. He asked to have the IV removed from his arm, which we did, and he refused to take any more medication. In the last couple days of his life no one but family members entered his room. The medical staff made themselves scarce.

As he severed himself more and more from the medical support system, his dependence on his family grew. I seemed able to calm him when he panicked, when he thrashed about on the bed, complaining of pain or his loss of self-control. It was Alex who helped me at these moments, explaining that all I needed to do was to place my hand lightly over my father's heart and stay in a peaceful place in my own mind by meditating. My father's body was no longer important; I had to address my attention to his spirit. This I did, and I was amazed at how well it went, calming him even more effectively than the hospital's pain drugs had done before he refused to take them any more.

Toward the second or third day, he had begun hallucinating, just as my friend the real estate woman had told me he would. The contents of these hallucinations were very meaningful, and very private, but not something I wish to pass along to the reader.

When I sought help with Dad's hallucinations, Alex told me, "Let your father have these illusions. Do whatever you can to confirm his reality, whatever that reality might be to him. The hallucinations are his only reality at this moment. Don't argue with him or try to convince him they aren't real, because to him they are real. If he seems frightened about them, ask him what you can do to help, and then do it, though it may require you to take action in a world that you cannot see. Just keep in mind that there are many realities that cannot be confirmed by the senses, and that is where you can be of the greatest service to your father now."

Following these instructions, I spent a good part of one day and most of another miming out little rituals such as straightening up a bookshelf that wasn't there, or scratching the toes of my father's left leg which had been amputated many years before. Some of these rituals were on the order of daily housekeeping; some went much deeper than that, communicating with people who weren't present (as far as I could determine), but who were playing out important dramas in Dad's life.

One of the most disturbing things to me was a recurring image when I sat beside my father with my hand on his heart. He would grow peaceful, almost blissful. Then an image would come into my mind of he and I in an invisible vehicle of some sort, racing out over a desert. My father appeared to be enjoying this—but I wasn't. The speed picked up, and the faster we went, the more nervous I became. Finally, I would jump, startled, and at that point I would leave my meditative space and my father would get agitated.

This experience happened several times. One afternoon my brother came to relieve me, and I drove back to my mother's house to rest. On the way back, I asked Alex what the ride in the invisible vehicle represented. He told me that it was Dad's image of his passage from life to death, and I had nothing to fear from it. I asked if this meant that my dream about the passage taking place in a boat had been wrong. Alex said no, it was not wrong, but everyone had his own image to symbolize his passage, and the boat was mine. The passage would be the same, he said, regardless of the vehicle involved.

I asked Alex what I should do about the startle reflex. He said only that I should go for a walk to a specific place I had often gone as a teenager. I was told exactly where to go, which was in a cedar swamp at the edge of the lake where I'd grown up.

It was in the dead of winter, and I had to borrow hiking boots and warm clothes to get where I was going. Directed by Alex, I came to a clearing in the woods and sat down on a fallen tree to wait. A few minutes later, I imagined that I saw a figure in a red hunting jacket coming toward me. Alex told me to greet this person and talk to him.

As the figure grew clearer in my mind, I realized that it was me, as a boy of sixteen. Though I was certain of this, I asked hin to identify himself. "I am the boy who came back from the dead," he said. "Don't you remember?"

He reminded me that when I was sixteen years old, I had contracted rabbit fever from a sick animal I had killed and eaten, and that I had been in a coma for a number of hours as a result. I had stood at that proverbial junction in the road between life and death, fully aware that the decision to live or die was completely up to me at that moment. I remember this experience very clearly, even to this day. There was no fear. Death seemed to pose no threat. I had made a choice to live only because it seemed right to me that to have done otherwise would have been a waste. There would, after all, come a time when I had no choice but to die, but until then I would choose life.

I asked The Boy Who Came Back From The Dead what he would do to help me. He said he didn't know, but that he would stay with me, and when the time came that he could help, he would let me know.

The next day, when I went back to visit my father at the hospital, he was much worse. Much of the time he lay very still, his eyes closed. When he did awaken for a second or two, he seemed not to connect with anything going on in the room. He frequently called me by another name, and when he did, I answered him as though I was that person. If he asked me to take care of something that wasn't there, I obeyed.

Most of the time, I sat by his bed and meditated. The image of the invisible vehicle carrying the two of us out over the desert was always there, but the ride seemed sane, and I did not grow frightened.

Toward evening, I became aware of my older brother coming into the room and just standing there, staring at my father. I was deep in meditation, and was concentrating on the image of the vehicle, hoping it wouldn't speed up and frighten me. I was clearly aware of the fact that the speed of the vehicle was gradually picking up, and there was nothing I could do about it.

The vehicle's speed was increasing by the second, so I finally asked for help from my inner guides. Alex appeared, simply looked at me, and then shrugged. He did not know what to do except to advise me to ask for help from The Boy Who Came Back From The Dead. Instantly, The Boy Who Came Back From the Dead appeared, saying that he could take my place in the vehicle now. He did this, and I watched as my father and he raced off. At that moment I felt relieved of a great burden, and I felt grounded and at peace.

It was early the next morning that my father died. He went in the most peaceful way imaginable, drifting off to sleep, never to awaken. But not before my older brother and I hugged him, told him that we loved him, and said goodbye.

Months after Dad died, my older brother described what had been going through his mind that evening when he entered the hospital room and stood so still, staring at Dad and I. My brother told me that he saw what appeared to be an ethereal copy of Dad's body floating above the bed, connected to the navel of the physical body below it by a thin, organic-looking thread. Nearly a year later, my brother discovered, quite by chance, that yogis report that this is a common experience, experienced by people close to a dying person, and that it represented the spirit leaving the physical body.

■

WHERE IS THE PROOF?

There is no way to confirm all these experiences, nor is it important to me that I do so now. The part that can be confirmed, however, is that my inner guides, mainly Alex and The Boy Who Came Back From The Dead, clearly served important functions that allowed me to be with my father in his last moments in ways that were helpful to him, to me, and to the entire family. Had I not sought and allowed myself to receive the help I got from these inner guides, the entire experience would have been an empty and confusing ordeal for all of us.

Alex, my dreams, and The Boy Who Came Back From The Dead helped on both spiritual and practical levels, I might add, providing as much counsel in arranging the funeral as they did in helping me understand how I should be with my father.

■

HOW TO WORK WITH DREAMS AND VISIONS

We all dream, and we all have visions. The same faculties that come into play during sleep—in which *imaginary experiences* take place—also play important roles in orienting us in space, and co-ordinating our physical actions during our waking hours. Without these faculties, we would not even be able to perform the simplest task. If we understand how these "dream" faculties work both during our waking and sleeping hours, we can also understand the great benefits we can derive from learning to work with these important aspects of our beings.

Let's begin with an explanation of how the "dreaming" faculties affect physical movement, since this will shed some light on the nature of how dreams affect our lives in even larger ways.

Neurophysiological research shows that all physical actions are organized inside the mind by an image of the person moving through space, just as it appears in your mind when you dream of yourself walking or running. Imagine, if you will, that there is a three-dimensional (holographic) movie constantly running in your mind, and that this movie acts as a "model" for your nervous system, sending signals to your muscles and organs as you walk across a room, run, sit, or lift your hand to turn the page of a book you're reading.

The organizing image (called a "mental hologram") is not only visual, but probably contains messages from all the senses, just as the physical body would be receiving in performing any actual physical movements. Most people are acutely aware of the visual aspects of the image, probably because of the importance of sight in daily life. But some are more aware of the tactile or aural or even taste and smell.

In recent years, entire new athletic training techniques have been developed around this principle. In the "mental training" of athletes and dancers, for example, significant performance improvements are achieved by "mentally rehearsing" the mental hologram, through visualizing the actions one is perfecting in addition to rehearsing the physical body. The world's greatest athletes and dancers have been found to be people who very early in life discovered how to rehearse in this way.

But of what value is this to us here? What does it have to do with dreams and visions? The answer is found by imagining that the path of one's entire life is guided in much the same way as physical movements are guided. Just as the mental hologram directs a single action occurring in the span of a split second, as in the case of lifting your hand to turn the page of a book, or over a period of minutes, as in the case of a dancer performing on the stage, so there are even more complex mental holograms that shape our lives, from birth to death. These complex holograms shape the ways we see the world, provide us with the raw material for making decisions and choices. The holograms are often the source of fears, anxieties, prohibitions, as well as personal attributes such as an aesthetic sense, an "ear" for music, a personal value system, and so forth.

People who work with dreams and visions become acutely aware of how the mental holograms, or other inner world experiences, affect their lives in the outer world. Jung devoted his life to the study of dreams, applying his scientific training to the examination of these phenomena in both ancient societies and modern life. His conclusion, of course, was that these ethereal experiences, the stuff of our unconscious minds, "chart the course" and "guide the rudder" of our daily lives, and without this activity of the inner world, we would indeed be like ships adrift on the seas, with no navigators or pilots.

Abraham Maslow stated it another way when he said that "man has his future within him, dynamically alive at this present moment." To know our dreams is to know the maps that guide our courses through life.

Can a person ever see the entire map? I have my doubts that we can, but my own experiences have convinced me that the occasional glimpse that we are allowed of the map (through dreams, visions, etc.), which is made more effective by skills such as those I describe in this book, can be tremendously helpful and comforting, especially during times of change, times of conflict, moments of grief, and times when our lives seem to have become static and lifeless.

The shaman would say that the person who has no skills for making contact with his dreams and visions is a person without self-power. Such a person might be compared to a ship's pilot who has no navigational skills, and who lacks even the most rudimentary knowledge about reading the stars to determine his course.

In the following few pages, I've described some simple tools for getting in touch with dreams and visions.

■

ACCESS TO THE INNER WORLD THROUGH DAYDREAMS

The value of daydreams is often overlooked, even by experts in the field. I consider daydreams important for several reasons, beginning with the fact that they are relatively accessible. These windows to the inner world are unique in that they are open during our conscious or waking states, offering opportunities to explore what's there and even make a record of what we find.

Most people daydream when they're bored or slightly anxious. For the person living in today's world, this is often when they're standing in line at the supermarket, or when stopped in freeway traffic. During such moments, we enter a state of consciousness which is comparable to a light trance. For an instant, the traffic around us or the long line of people at the checkout counter fades away, and we enter a private world where we experience a vacation trip we'd like to take, or the resolution of a problem we've been facing for a long time, or how it will feel to drive the new car we're planning to buy, or how the house will look when we finish remodeling it. And, let's not forget one of the most common daydreams of all—replaying an argument or discussion we've had in the recent past, this time inserting all the things we *should have said* the first time around.

Dream research shows that dreams and visions are most active and intense during times of major change, especially associated with stressful but happy events such as: graduation from college; anticipation of marriage; the beginning of a new project; a promotion in your career; or when you are on the verge of making a decision that will change the way you have been living your life. Daydreams and visions will also be particularly active under less happy, stressful circumstances: with a death in the family; with the failure of a business; with the loss of a job; with the separation from a loved one; or with divorce.

When you encounter periods of change or challenge, remind yourself that this is a time when your dreams and visions will be particularly intense and accessible. Then, when you're in situations such as I've described above— stuck in traffic, waiting in line at the checkout counter— pay attention to the images that flow through your mind. As your mind drifts, let it go. But follow it at a respectable distance with your *observer mind.* The observer mind is that part of you that watches or even makes mental notes of what you are doing, even as you are doing it. It is the part that alerts you to the fact that it's now your turn at the checkout counter, or that traffic is at last moving ahead and it is time for you to take action. It is also the part that judges you, that stands back and says, "Now, that was a really stupid thing to do!" or "Hey, that was pretty good! You did that well." It is also that part of you which notes, "A moment ago I was a hundred miles away, imagining how it would feel to bask in the sun on a beach of white sand! Now the traffic is moving and I must pay attention to driving my car."

Let that observer part of your self look back and note in a conscious way the daydream you were just having. Say to yourself, "I was daydreaming that I was..." and then fill in the blanks: "...basking in the sun on a beautiful white beach in Bermuda;" or "I was daydreaming that I was telling my boss that I would like to apply for the new position opening in the marketing department;" or whatever it is you were daydreaming.

It is best if you can write down what you were daydreaming, even if it is a two or three word reminder to yourself. Later, sit down and look more closely at your vision. Here are some questions you might ask as you do this:

- Where were you in the daydream? Can you name one aspect of the imagined physical surroundings? Can you describe those surroundings in greater detail?

- Were you alone? If you were not alone, who was with you? What relationship did you have to these people?

- What action were you engaged in? What were you doing in the dream or vision?

95

- What general attitude did you have? Were you relaxed? Open and loving? Were you in conflict with your environment or with someone in that environment? Were you at peace with yourself? Were you in a position of power? Were you a victim? Were you a passive observer?

- Were you faced with a challenge? If so, what was the outcome?

- How did the dream or vision end?

- How did you feel immediately after the dream ended?

Sometimes, of course, a daydream or vision consists of only a single image. If it is a vivid image, write down a description of it as soon as you can. Keep the description in a notebook where you can refer to it from time to time. Here are some suggestions for working with such images:

- Is this a brand new image for me, or is it something that has come up before? If it is a recurring image, assume that it plays a role in the complex mental hologram that guides your everyday life. Ask what the image means to you, and make notes on any associations you have with it.

- In the normal course of a day, recall your image and ask what, if any, associations you make between that image and your present activity. Sometimes the image will evoke no associations whatsoever. At other times the image will be rich with meaning, providing clues about the role that image plays in the complex hologram that guides your life.

- Ask people who know you well what they make of the image. Do they see it as reflecting special interests, worries, or aspirations that you frequently express to them?

- Look for ways that this image relates to memories you may have of the past.

- Strike up an imaginary dialogue with the image, especially if it is a living thing—an animal, a person, or even a "personified" object. Ask it what it is doing in your life. You may be very surprised by its answers. Ask it how it might be of service to you. Ask if its influence in your life is positive or negative. If negative, you can literally tell it to go away and stop bothering you.

Work with the image just as you might do if the real object or animal or person represented by the image appeared in your life. Talk to it, examine it, get to know it.

At this point you might say, "Okay, once I've done that, where do I go with this information?" The answer is that your own work with the daydream or image will dictate what actions if any, you will take. Sometimes the answer is "do nothing." Sometimes your answer comes in the form of solid determination to change something in your life, or to work harder at accomplishing a goal you've decided is very important to you.

Ultimately, my answer to the question about what one should do with the information received from dreams and visions is really quite simple: Treat the vision or daydream as a "real" experience. Just as it is true that some *real* experiences call for action and some don't, so that same principle is true of imagined experience. You will know when there is a call for action and when there isn't. Dreams and visions are infrequently clear answers to puzzles.

■

97

ADOPT THE ATTITUDE OF AN ADVENTURER

It is best to think of your development of the ability to be in touch with your dreams and visions as something akin to building bridges between your inner world (the unconscious) and your outer world (consciousness). To carry that metaphor further, it is as though the inner and outer worlds are two cities, and these two cities are highly interdependent. People go back and forth between these two places constantly, affecting changes that are never wholly predictable. Because of the complex exchanges which take place between the two cities, it is important to take a stroll now and then, crossing the bridge to explore the way the people live on *the other side*.

By knowing our *neighbors* on the *other side* (from our inner world), by simply strolling through their streets and talking with the people we meet there, we are better able to understand and accept some of the changes that occur in our own city (our conscious world) as a result of our interdependencies.

Jung and many other psychologists, as well as shamans, say that the unconscious mind may be even more important than consciousness. The unconscious mind shapes the way we make sense of the world and directs our decisions in ways that are far more complex than the classic logic that we would like to believe guides our major decisions. In light of this, we begin to see how the bridges to the unconscious not only satisfy our curiosity, they allow us to make visits to the *navigator's office* where we can peruse the charts and become familiar with relationships, symbols, and situations that will affect our lives.

■

ORACULAR TECHNIQUES FOR GETTING IN TOUCH WITH DREAMS AND VISIONS

For a more deliberate and systematic way of looking at your dreams and visions, I suggest working with one of the many *oracle* systems that are available. This might be the ancient *I-Ching,* or the *Runes,* or the *Tarot* cards, or *Star + Gate,* or my own system, *Mind Jogger,* or any other system of oracle that appeals to you. I don't recommend one system over the other because I think it is important to choose one with which you feel comfortable. I look upon oracle systems as tools, in this case mental tools.

In choosing any tool, it is important that you have one that *fits* you; no matter how a tool is praised by other people, no matter how much it costs or how popular it is, you will use it effectively in your own life only if it fits you, only if you *feel right with it.*

There are many ways to use the oracles. Depending on who you're talking to, the oracle can be a way of looking into the future or a way of simply reading your own mind. My own belief is that the oracle does both; it allows you to look into the future because it helps you look into your own inner world. I agree with Maslow that "the future lies within us," and most oracles give you a glimpse of how your future would look at any given moment if you simply allow yourself to reflexively follow the "chart" you find there. The wonderful thing about developing skills for looking at the charts is that when you can do this you gain self-power in making decisions that allows you to reap the greatest benefits from those charts.

Here's the way I recommend that you work with the oracle of your choice:

■

ORACLE INSTRUCTIONS

Preliminaries: Become familiar with your chosen system's way of selecting the cards or readings it contains.

Familiarize yourself with any symbols or readings the system offers.

Set up a diary or notebook for your work with the oracle.

Then follow the format described below:

1. Begin by stating a question or describing a problem you wish to solve. You might also wish to describe a fragment of a dream or vision that you want either to recall more fully or better understand. The first part of the description can be as emotional or even as negative as you wish. It is important, however, to finish the description of the problem with a positive statement about the outcome you would desire. Students of human nature have repeatedly demonstrated that "Negative statements tend to create walls against solutions while positive statements create doors and windows." For example, a person might begin with a description of how they hate their job, want their boss to get off their case, and of how agitated they feel every morning when the alarm clock reminds them it is time to go to work. They end the description of their problem with a positive statement such as: "I want to figure out what I can do so that I can enjoy my work."

2. You will make three selections in all:

THE SOURCE READING

In this reading you explore the possible causes or sources of the problem. Where did it begin? What influenced the situation so that it became problematic? When did the central image of your dream first appear in your life?

THE OBSTRUCTION READING

In this reading you explore the possibility that there is something about the present situation or the distressing or puzzling dream image which, although uncomfortable or painful, satisfies a special need in your inner life. In order to change the situation you don't like and begin to understand the solutions that are offered, you will need to identify what that benefit is and let it go. For example, a person realizes that their job is not challenging enough but feels "safe" in doing it because their full potential is never put to the test. Or they have recurring dreams in which an authority figure stops them from doing something they want to do. The obstruction reading would guide them in identifying that aspect of the problem and they could then make a choice about giving up that "safety" or keeping it.

THE SOLUTION READING

In this reading you explore possible solutions.

3. Select your first oracle reading by whatever method is recommended in the system you have chosen to use. For example, if you are using the I-Ching, you would throw the coins or yarrow sticks and make your first selection.

Carefully read and think about each oracle reading. Then consider which part of the reading you're working on—Source, Obstruction, or Solution. Ask yourself, "What do I *associate* with this reading that would tell me about the Source (or Obstruction, or Solution) of this problem?" In other words, what comes to your mind, telling you something about the Source or Obstruction or Solution, as you read the oracle you've selected? What does it tell me about the dream or the problem I'm working on?

This associative process is important. Do not attempt to *interpret* what the oracle reading says. Simply record what comes to your mind. In this respect, the oracle is serving an *evocative* role, making suggestions that help you cross the bridge to visit your unconscious mind, so that you can make use of your own inner resources. You take a look at one or more of the numerous elements of the mental hologram that guides your life.

Whatever comes up will be useful. Don't worry that it doesn't sound profound, or that it seems like common sense. The "truth" you seek will frequently present itself in that way; people who are strongly intuitive identify the feeling of a well focused intuitive insight as "common place," or as "a feeling of ease and normalcy that is, nevertheless, quietly and comfortably exciting."

YOUR MOST IMPORTANT INSIGHT

After working with the readings, record the most important insight you've received thus far. This may be as simple or as complex as you wish.

MOST IMMEDIATE ACTION

It is finally through our actions that we let ourselves be known—both to ourselves and to others. I therefore recommend that you make a statement about an immediate action you can take to implement the discoveries you've made by the above process, manifesting them as actions in the *real* world. This need not be a hugely ambitious action. I am reminded of a woman who desperately wanted to improve her work situation. She determined to do this, and the most immediate action she could think to take was to buy a beautiful cut glass vase and put a flower on her desk. She did this and thereafter made a point of always bringing a fresh flower to work, cut from the yard where she lived. Though a simple gesture, the flower brightened her life and became a positive reminder of her desire to make career changes. In time she did reach her career goals, and she said that the decision to keep a flower on her desk had been a crucial beginning step for her.

LONG TERM GOALS

This last part of the process may or may not apply to every question you process in this way. But with larger, more complex situations, you may require a statement of both an immediate action you might take and your long term goals to make an important change in your life.

■

The associations you make in the above work with oracles may or may not appear as single, coherent visions or daydreams. For many people, the visions will immediately be translated into words. For example, if you select a Tarot card with the image of harmony and balance, you might make an association with a time in your past when you felt completely at ease and happy with yourself. You might choose simply to write a description of that moment: "I was skiing at Bear Mountain, and on the last run of the day everything fell into place. It was a beautiful, graceful run, and my body and mind felt perfectly in tune with each other and with the run. At the bottom of the hill I had a tremendous sense of power and confidence." You might then go on to write how that might apply to the Source, Obstruction, or Solution—depending on which phase of the process you're working on at that time. For example, you might write: "It is this kind of harmony with everything in my life that I would like to bring into the problem situation."

On the other hand, although you might be recalling that experience of harmony or self-power in your past, you would not be able to describe the actual scene that was the source of your feelings, but would go straight to verbalizing it: "I recall how it has felt in my past to be balanced and at ease, but I'm so far away from that now! I know I'm capable of doing it again, but how?"

Think of the oracle as an evocative tool rather than as a fortune-telling system. That is, after all, how the ancients intended most of these systems to be used. The discovery of images or other personal resources that are evoked by the readings are your own material, the charts that are unique to your life. They are the source of your self-power. Don't mistake them for anything else.

■

SYNCHRONICITY IN ORACLES

Oracles very often reflect what Jung called "synchronicity," that is, meaningful coincidences that have no perceivable common causal relationships. For example, dreams, visions, or oracle readings can have a correspondence with external reality. Jung himself studied the I-Ching for this very reason, and was responsible, along with his friend Richard Wilhelm, for getting a translation of this book of ancient wisdom published in Europe. He said of the I-Ching,

> *Are the I-Ching's answers meaningful or not? If they are, how does the connection between psychic and physical sequence of events come about? Time and again I encountered amazing coincidences which seemed to suggest the idea of an acausal parallelism (synchronicity)... it became quite clear that a significant number of answers did indeed hit the mark.*

■

THE SIMPLE SECRETS OF DREAMWORK

One of the main difficulties people face in working with dreams is recalling them. Recalling dreams is really a matter of getting into the habit of doing so, and of providing yourself with the proper tools.

You begin by keeping a dream journal and a pen beside your bed at all times. Or, you may prefer to use a small, personal tape recorder. The important thing is that you need to be able to record your dreams, and if these tools aren't readily available at your bedside, the chances are good that you'll never recall a single dream.

When you awaken in the morning, immediately pick up your journal and try to recall any dreams you've had—even if it is only a fragment of a dream. In the beginning you may be able to recall only general themes, such as being in a conflict with someone. But you may not be able to recall your adversary's identity, where the conflict took place, or how it eventually came out. The following checklist, describing the sequence in which most dreams occur, will assist you in recalling your own dreams:

1. WHERE IT OCCURRED: Describe in as much detail as possible where the dream began. For example, "I was walking down the street in New York City..."

2. WHO WAS THERE WITH YOU? Describe or name any people who were with you—if any. For example, "Jim, my old college roommate, was with me..."

3. EXPOSITION: Describe details about the scene of action. For example, "We were just getting ready to cross a street when a car stopped in front of us, the driver rolled down the window, and Jim and I recognized the face of his ex-wife, Melody..."

4. DEVELOPMENT: Describe what happened next. For example, "Melody didn't recognize us right away. She asked us directions for getting to the public library. I said, is that you, Melody? And she answered that she couldn't remember her name..."

106

5. CULMINATION: Describe how the action is resolved or how the dream ends. For example, "Jim then said, it is you, Melody! Neither one of us had seen her in nearly twenty years. But she denied this, insisting that she didn't know either of us."

6. RESOLUTION: Describe the final scene. For example, "Without warning the car suddenly pulled away. Jim and I looked at each other in bewilderment. We were certain we had seen Melody, and we felt a compelling need to track her down. It was as though we both had something urgent to tell her."

In the beginning you may be able to recall only bits and pieces of your dreams. Don't worry about this. Keep working with your dreams, writing down as much or as little detail as you can recall each time. You will find that with persistence you will soon be recalling your dreams in great detail.

■

DREAM INTERPRETATION

How should you "interpret" your dreams? I would have to agree with Jung that it is "important not to have any preconceived, doctrinaire opinions about the statements made by dreams." I have never found it fruitful to use dream interpretation books that are available in many bookstores these days. In fact, I would warn you against using such books. Although there are some so-called universal symbols that appear in dreams, dreams themselves are comprised of a highly individualized language of symbols and meanings, unique to the dreamer. Even though your dream might contain a universal symbol, the ways in which symbols can be individualized are almost unlimited.

When I was in my twenties, I went to a Freudian analyst who helped me work with my dreams. In the beginning, I made much progress, learning a great deal about the way my inner life went together. Then, as our analysis of my dreams became more and more detailed, we got bogged down. All too often my analyst's interpretations simply didn't fit. Both of us agreed that the difficulty I was having was not a matter of resistance. Finally, I had a dream in which I saw my dreams being played out on a huge round stage. I was in the audience talking to the actors via a telephone. The play being enacted was entirely my own script. Not only that, I had produced and directed the play.

With the final act there was much applause. But, as people came up to congratulate me, they expressed puzzlement. One of them told me, "It was a wonderful production, and I feel that I understand it. But what language were the actors speaking?"

In working with this dream I realized for the first time that dreams communicated on both a universal and a private level. I might, for example, be emotionally moved by the distress of a man stranded on a rock in the middle of the ocean—even though the language he spoke as he cried out for help was completely foreign to my ears. Thus, the stage production I created in my dream moved people in the audience, connecting on that universal level, but contained language and symbols that only I understood.

The dream of my theater production also taught me that I create everything that occurs in my dreams. I had to take full responsibility for the events that unfolded there.

From then on, my analyst asked me what I thought various symbols meant in my dreams. By following my interpretations of these symbols—sometimes with prompting from my analyst—we began to move forward again. My individualized interpretations of the symbols led to understandings that both of us agreed would never have otherwise occurred.

■

RELIVE YOUR DREAMS TO UNDERSTAND THEIR MESSAGES

I believe that one of the most productive ways of working with dreams is this: In a fully awake state, read the dream you have recorded and fill in anything you feel is missing. Then put yourself into the middle of the dream. Pretend that you are living it out once more in your imagination. For example, if you have dreamed that you are driving across a desert in your car, put yourself there. Imagine that you are behind the wheel of that car. Then start looking around and asking questions. Here are some sample possibilities:

• Ask what you are doing driving across the desert.

• Ask whose car you are driving, and what circumstances are behind your having it.

• Ask what your mission is (if it isn't already apparent from your dream).

• Let's say you stop at a gas station where there is a sign

advertising a hotel in a town a thousand miles away. Ask what the sign means to you.

Explore the dream as though you know nothing about it, as though you haven't even the vaguest notion what it is all about. After asking questions, wait for answers to come. Be patient.

If there are people in the dream, strike up conversations with them. In your imagination, ask them what business they have with you. Treat them as if they were real people. Play in this imaginary world. Remember, it is your territory, solely yours, and you can do whatever you wish to do here.

There are no right or wrong questions or answers when it comes to working with your dreams in this way. Sometimes your explorations will turn up valuable insights for you. Sometimes they will turn up utter nonsense. Sometimes a dream will begin to make sense to you, or reveal something about your inner world to you only years after you've recorded it and puzzled over it.

Remember that your goal is not to crack the mystery of every dream but simply to make contact with your inner world. The quality of communication that you establish with the "land and geography" of your inner world is what is important. The fact that you are able to find the path into it, and visit it, become familiar with it, link up with what goes on there in the same way that you familiarize yourself with the streets and the shops and the town where you live—that's what's important.

■

SOMETIMES THERE IS NO MYSTERY AT ALL

Don't forget that sometimes the dream or vision is quite literal and doesn't require even the lightest prob-ing. Kekule's vision of the closed ring, for example, was a straight-forward answer to a question he had been ask-ing. I am also reminded of a dream that Jung reported in his memoirs: He dreamed that a friend, who was dead, came to him and told him to go to his (the friend's) library. He described the exact location of a book, which Jung would reach by standing on a stool. The book was the second from the left of a series of five books bound in red leather. Jung had never been to his friend's library, and did not know what to expect. However, he made a call to his friend's widow on the pretense that he wished to borrow a book.

Jung went to the library, followed the directions he'd received in his dream, and located the aforemen-tioned book. Although the book contained no informa-tion he could use, the title suggested a definite answer to a problem Jung had been struggling with at the time he had the dream.

The bottom line is this: When you're working with dreams and visions, begin with the simplest and the most obvious interpretations. As often as not they are as *literal* as life in your waking state. Especially consider a literal interpretation when there is no particular emotional charge, or no physical or emotional danger or hardship in carrying out what the dream or vision seems to suggest.

I am here reminded of a comment attributed to the master of dream symbolism himself. Being an avid cigar-smoker, he was once asked about its phallic symbolism. He removed the cigar, studied it for a moment, and replied: "Sometimes a cigar is just a cigar."

Dreams are not infallible messengers; treat them with the same skepticism or critical mind that you would a message from a friend or acquaintance. As in working with inner guides, keep the principle in mind that "dreams, after all, are only human."

CHAPTER FOUR:

Fetiches

There is a small, almost comical figure that sits on top of my computer monitor. It is a Zuni fetich, a figure of a fox carved in gray stone, a fox with a bushy tail and red heartline, the characteristic heartline arrow running straight and clean from the tip of his nose to his heart.

For the Zuni, the fetich was a powerful source of wisdom, a way of accessing ancient knowledge about the hunt as well as about *medicine*. On its most practical level, it was a way to explore the inner world, the world of wisdom and power that existed in the human spirit. Anthropologist Tom Bahti describes the purpose of fetiches within the Zuni culture; they were intended to:

> *. . . assist man, that most vulnerable of all living creatures, in meeting the problems that face him during his life. Each fetich contains a living power, which, if treated properly and with veneration will give its help to its owner.*

Should a desired result fail to be attained the fetich is not at fault but the person who conducted the ceremony is. Either he offended the fetich (perhaps by failing to feed it ceremoniously) or was not of 'good heart' when he asked for its assistance.

On its most practical level, the Zuni fetich was a contemplative tool, a reference point for exploring and keeping one's attention focused on the wisdom of the tribe.

The Zuni was a hunter, and his whole life revolved around the hunt. Thus, the "prey fetiches," as they were called, were always animals, either the animals the tribe hunted or the animals with whom they shared their prey. (The Mountain Lion, for example, was the master hunter. Though the Zuni seldom hunted him, he served as a model for the person who wanted to emulate his great hunting skills.) On a deeper level, the fetich was a spiritual tool, representing essential powers that the animal possessed, powers that were used by the shaman or medicine man to heal disease or solve problems.

It was believed that everything in the universe, be it animal, human, river, lightning, the earth itself, or even rock, had its own spirit. So the fetich of a fox would contain not only the spirit of the fox but also the spirit of rock and of the person who crafted the fetich. It is interesting to note that the earliest fetiches were not crafted by people but were rocks or pieces of wood shaped by nature. It was believed that the rocks or wood were shaped by the same forces that shaped the actual animal they represented. Later, when men began shaping rocks, crafting small figures from stone, it was believed that fetiches made in this way were less powerful than those shaped by nature. However, since it was believed that man was given that power to create fetiches by the ultimate Creator, the products of his efforts—that is, the fetiches he shaped—were considered to have value commensurate with the powers with which the craftsman had been endowed by his creator.

It is not difficult to imagine the hunter working with his fetich before a hunt. The experienced hunter, silently contemplating the stone image of his prey, would undoubtedly have had hundreds of images of previous hunts called up in his mind. His full attention would be focused on his prey, and he would be reminded of everything he knew of that activity. All such knowledge would bring the spirit of the animal into his consciousness, until finally the hunter was fully primed for the hunt.

There are many explanations for the function of fetiches down through history, with small figures of animals or people acting as tools for accessing wisdom not only for the hunt but for virtually every other matter of the human spirit. Psychologist Julian James had speculated that figures such as this served to focus the spiritual attention of those who followed the religious traditions to which they belonged. At one time, James believes, such figures may have *spoken* to the devout in the form of "hallucinated voices."

■

THE FETICH AS A MENTAL HOLOGRAM

It is my belief that in modern times fetiches can serve as *templates* for creating meaningful mental holograms. Let me first reiterate what mental holograms are:

Technically, a hologram is a three-dimensional figure created entirely of light. The technology for them was developed by Dennis Gabor, who won a Nobel prize for his work in 1971. Unlike a fetich, the hologram has no substance and yet, projected in space, it produces what the viewer takes to be a solid form. One can walk around the hologram and view it from any angle.

In the 1920s, the research of Karl Lashley began to suggest that the brain used something like holograms to organize certain complex information, and that each brain cell, regardless of its more specific functions, also functioned almost like a piece of holographic film. This suggested that each cell had an imprint of the whole brain and all the information it contained, and because of this one part of the brain could take over functions of another not because that new section could be retrained, but because it already knew.

Although this theory interested brain researchers, Lashley's research remained obscure until only the past couple of decades. Recently, researchers have taken a new look at his work, and have even expanded his theories. In his book *Toward a Science of Consciousness*, Kenneth Pelletier suggests that the hologram "serves as a neurophysiological model in which brain function is potentially distributed throughout each cell of the brain."

Similarly, Karl Pribram, a brain researcher at Stanford University, believes that a three-dimensional image, which might best be envisioned as a kind of hologram, serves to organize information in the mind. For example, the images we produce in our mind's eye, of the first car we owned, or of the house where we lived as a child, are holographic rather than two-dimensional in nature. Of course, they are produced by the energies of the human consciousness rather than light, but the effects are similar.

It is believed that the holographic principle is what allows us to organize the incredibly complex muscular responses required to walk, run, or perform athletic feats. To do these things, we spontaneously create mental holograms that move, and these tell every muscle in the body what to do.

Holograms, Pribram and others argue, are necessary for such complex action because only with a three-dimensional image is it possible to coordinate all areas of the body at once. The Soviets, who have developed sophisticated mental training techniques for their athletes based on this theory, believe that the hologram created in the athlete's mind also includes the inner organs and the senses.

I mention this to suggest the great complexity of the mental hologram, and the all but infinite number of pieces of information that might be organized through a single hologram. Remember, the hologram not only has height and width and depth, it has volume, an inside and an outside, and since it is in effect transparent, it also has the ability to make instant associations or connections between any elements contained therein, regardless of where they are attached to the hologram.

You can easily test this theory for yourself. At this

moment, picture in your mind's eye the first car you ever owned. Look at it from the front. From the back. From the side. Now take a look at what's under the hood or in the glove compartment or in the trunk. Notice how in your mind's eye the car has volume. Moreover, taking a look in the glove compartment probably doesn't require your opening the door of the car, then leaning over to open the glove compartment. You go immediately into the glove compartment.

Even with this rather concrete image of the car, you are using the mental hologram to organize millions of pieces of information. If you are mechanically minded and you had worked on the car, you could look at things about the engine or tires or transmission that no one could have seen on the surface of the real car. Moreover, as you hold the image of the car in your mind, you'll probably discover that it also brings forth many other memories associated with the car: a trip you took, a lover you had when you owned the car, or the year you had trouble keeping up the payments because you were unemployed.

The hologram of the car is created not simply by your willful efforts to construct such an image. Rather, it is made up of billions of bits and pieces of your experiences around that car, most of which you probably can't even trace because they exist at the subtlest, subliminal levels. The experiences are recorded there through messages from all the senses—sight, sound, the feeling of movement, touch, smell—as well as intellectual and emotional memories.

When you happen to see a car going down the street that is the same make and model as the car you once owned, your mental hologram may well be referenced.

In this respect, the external car—the one you happen to see going down the street—acts as a "template", that is, it provides a kind of mental mold for shaping the hologram in your mind.

Fetiches work like templates, too, shaping holograms that you may have in your mind. For example, the Zuni hunter's fetich of a bear acts as a template shaping the mental hologram he has of the bear. And, with the bear hologram in place, all the billions of pieces of experiential information he has had, or which his fellow tribesmen have had around the subject of bears, suddenly become accessible to him.

The beauty of the template, which the fetich provides, is that it is solid and focused. It can hold the person's attention—that is, maintain the specific mental hologram in place for a long period of time. This gives the hunter or other person consulting the fetich plenty of time to study his subject.

Now let's add still another dimension to this model of the power of fetiches. In the introduction to this book I used a quote from the German physicist Ludwig Boltzman, who suggests that mental activity follows the same laws as quantum physics. The elementary particles and the patterns of energy activated by the mental hologram interact with the universe in ways we cannot even fully imagine. Thus, the magic of the fetich reported by the Zuni in ancient times may contain more than a hint of truth. The powerful focus of mental energy produced through the fetich and its hologram is, indeed, important to consider.

I have an image of mental holograms as being like magnets that you hold out into the environment, which attract elemental particles that are floating around out

121

there, and which have forms similar to your hologram. Likewise, one's own holograms are like transmitters, sending out patterns of energy that can be pulled in by another person's mental holograms halfway around the world. But this is highly speculative. What is less speculative is the effect of fetiches and mental holograms on "attention," that is, on alerting us to information concerning that hologram in our immediate environment.

■

HOW FETICHES HELP RECALL COMPLEX INFORMATION

Fetiches and mental holograms not only organize complex experiences for us, they also alert us to more information, related to the fetich, from the external environment. There is no great mystery about how or why this works. If we have a strong image in our mind of a fox, a particular car, or anything else, that mental image focuses our attention and tells us to be on the alert for any new information that might be added to that hologram.

For me, the fetich that sits on top of my computer monitor triggers my mental hologram of foxes. I look at the fetich as I write, and I recall my experiences with foxes in the Michigan woods where I grew up. Families of foxes lived in the cedar swamps that circled the lake near my boyhood home. The swamps were impenetrable in the summer, but when winter came, freezing over the wet ground, one could venture in. In my mind, I am shivering with cold as I enter the edge of the swamp. The marshy ground has donned a veil of ice, the trees have shed their leaves, now coated with frost. And then I see the red blur of the fox galloping over the rough floor of the swamp, its bright fur a sharp contrast to the black shadows cast by the trees and bogs, and the white snow blanketing it all.

The fox intrigues me. I am attracted to this figure—whether carved in rock or the real thing. Sometimes, he is like a beacon or a guide for me, leading me into the shadowy inner world. Sometimes his role is much more mundane than that. When I drive down the street in my car, with the image of the fox fetich in my mind, I am much more likely to notice fox images in the environment than I otherwise might see. I notice the fox on the logo of a local film developing laboratory; I notice the bumper sticker on the car in front of me that says "Foxy Grandma Driving;" and in the bookstore I pick up a children's book on foxes that I might otherwise never have noticed.

■

CREATIVE POTENTIALS AND FETICHES

Since the Age of Reason, we have had at our disposal excellent tools for sorting and selecting bits of information from our inner and outer worlds. Mathematics, language, a thousand and one technological systems—all help us pull information cleanly and accurately out of that enormous warehouse of our minds. We do this in the service of simplicity, and in the service of gaining control over our lives. There is, of course, no fault in this; much is accomplished that could otherwise not be accomplished. But confining ourselves to the tools that only do that is a little like the carpenter who owns a huge box of tools but never uses anything but a hammer and saw.

It is my belief that mental holograms, and the fetiches that we use as templates for them, hold the key to gaining access to the inner world without cutting away the rich associative processes that go along with them. With the hologram intact, we draw in possibilities that cannot be anticipated. This is the epitome of creativity. The hologram, rather than sorting and selecting, or narrowing down the possibilities, does something quite the opposite—"opening out a way, whence the imprisoned splendor may escape," as Robert Browning put it.

Because of the nature of the human mind, mental materials organized around holograms (and perhaps suggested by the fetiches we choose) intermingle, making infinite associations between bits and pieces of information. And out of these vast warehouses of information there constantly arise new possibilities for solving problems, for discovering entirely new human capabilities.

■

HOW TO USE FETICHES

Any single fetich has a degree of specificity, an individual identity that is like no other. For example, a bear fetich looks like a bear and a fox fetich looks like a fox. And because they have specific identities even beyond that, determined by the artisan who made it or the experiences of the person who uses it, each one will elicit a different set of thoughts, feelings, and ideas. A bear fetich evokes the spirit of the bear, the fox the spirit of the fox, etc. Along with each evocation comes information specific to that spirit: the fox evokes thoughts and memories of experiences related to the fox. The bear evokes thoughts and memories of experiences related to the bear.

According to Zuni mythology, as reported by Frank Hamilton Cushing in a study originally published by the U.S. Government printing office in 1883, every fetich has a complex character, based on that society's mythology.

I have other fetiches with which I regularly work, and each one of them has a distinctly different character or identity:

I have a small coyote fetich, carved of a light green rock, with an abalone shell arrowhead attached to his back with a turn of monofilament fishline. Coyote is a somewhat comical character, which I compare to the classic fool of Elizabethan drama who spoke in riddles but always shed great light on any problem. He also evokes thoughts of the California Indians' "Coyote stories," stories of a legendary figure who is portrayed as being part god, and part fool. When I first began working with coyote, he told me that he was in my life to teach me that wisdom should be viewed as a "weapon," with equal potentials for doing good or harm. He told me he would teach me how to carry my wisdom with grace.

I also have a fetich which is an antique silver button in the shape of a Thunderbird. My mother purchased it at a trading post in New Mexico in the 1920s and gave it to me nearly fifty years later. The bird has a bead of turquoise in the middle of its breast, with arrows and Indian swastikas on its wings. It was made by Navajos, and the symbols on its wings represent lightning and something that would roughly be translated as *pure energy.* I call this fetich "Bird," and it brings up images for me of an airborn spirit or the life force of living things. Although he is able to sail freely in the heavens, he is also very connected with the earth, and it is in the tension between earth and sky that he finds his power. He is a powerful spiritual image for me.

■

CHOOSING FETICHES AND ESTABLISHING INDIVIDUAL CHARACTER

I cannot emphasize strongly enough the importance of getting to know and recognize each fetich as an individual character or *persona* before you sit down to work with them. Here's how I recommend you do that:

Choose fetiches to which you feel strongly attracted. If possible, begin with objects that have been in your life for a considerable period of time. I do not necessarily recommend working with Zuni fetiches unless you do feel an attachment to them. I believe they are effective for me because each of them has a special meaning for me, and most of them were objects that were in my life for a long time and toward which I felt an attachment, long before I began to use them in this way.

A fetich can be any object toward which you feel a strong affection or attachment. It might be a Victorian figurine given to you by a favorite aunt when you were five years old. It might be an autographed baseball. It might be a stuffed toy such as a teddy bear, or even a photograph of a person or place.

■

DON'T UNDERSTAND YOUR FETICHES TOO QUICKLY

Take a great deal of time with your fetiches in the beginning stage. If possible, carry your fetich around with you for a number of days. Get to know it in a variety of circumstances. Set the fetich on your desk at work. Put him or her on the dashboard of your car. Place it on the table beside your bed. Carry on internal dialogues with them. Ask them their names, what they consider to be their most valuable traits, and how they think they can serve you.

Each of my fetiches has a long history for me. Except for one, all came to me as gifts. Some have been with me for fifteen years or more, one for over thirty years.

An important part of the character of each fetich can be the personal history you share with it. For example, in working with the Tomahawk Head, which is one of my fetiches, I can go back in time and in my mind's eye see the place where I found it when I was sixteen years old. I recall how cold it was that day, the terrain around me, the size of the tree against which I leaned, how I reached down with my left hand and felt the tomahawk head fill my hand under its light snow covering.

I recall the various places where I had put the tomahawk head over the years: how it had felt in the pocket of my hunting jacket as I walked back to the car with it the day I found it; how it had sat on the window-sill of the bedroom I'd had as a teenager; how it had moved from one place to another as I moved about over the years...Millions of memories, thoughts, and feelings, millions of images from my past, are evoked by that piece of carved stone.

I can also recall numerous "consultations" I have had with the inner guide who is associated with this object. These have come over the past six to eight years.

I cannot emphasize strongly enough the importance of choosing fetiches to which you feel powerfully drawn, and with whom you feel that you share a personal history. We choose objects in our lives, and we keep some objects while discarding others, because they connect with something deep and important inside us. Every object for which we feel a strong personal attachment is a potential "channel," a key unlocking the door to our inner resources.

■

EDUCATING YOUNG FETICHES Sometimes it is necessary to create a history for a fetich. This was certainly the case for me when I got my Mountain Lion fetich. I was reading about fetiches at the time—my first study of them coming nearly fifteen years after I received my first one as a gift—and found that Mountain Lion was considered to be a key prey fetich. I asked my fetiches what they thought about this, and they agreed that to complete their circle, they would need to have Mountain Lion join them.

I did not know exactly what to do about this. I had never tried to buy a fetich before, since all of mine were given to me as gifts. But a short time after I made the decision to get one, I noticed an Indian artifact store in a shopping center where I'd gone to have lunch with a business associate. I went inside and found exactly the fetich I wanted.

When I got the Mountain Lion home, however, he seemed like an alien to the other fetiches, and I felt that they were simply not going to let me use him. At last, I asked the other fetiches what was going on. They told me that the new fetich had no history. At this point it had little more personal identity than being a curio made on an Indian reservation for the tourist trade.

I carried Mountain Lion around with me for several weeks in order to "educate" him, give him a history. I had dialogues with him, but these always seemed fabricated and uninteresting. No matter what I did, the other fetiches wouldn't accept him, and I didn't feel inspired or even interested by his presence. The fetiches finally told me to take Mountain Lion out to a wilderness area, that this was the only way that he could ever create a history for himself.

And so, one summer afternoon I drove out to the country and placed Mountain Lion in an oak tree overlooking a wilderness area. In the weeks ahead I would go out to visit him from time to time. Or I would simply think about him, try to see the world through his eyes. After several weeks I went out and picked him up. This time, when I brought him back to the circle with the other fetiches, he indeed had a personal history. He knew a great deal about issues that had to do with hunting boundaries and the divisions between the civilized world and the wilderness, which I'll go into with greater detail in a moment.

Here is the first dialogue I had with him following

this education in the wilderness:

"You placed me on a line between wilderness and civilization," he said. "On my side of the road there were open fields, and hunting was good. On the other side of the road there were houses. I am a very territorial animal, and recognizing this line between civilization and the wild was important to me. What is survival and balance on my side of the road is viewed as brutal on the other. I hunt and kill what I need for my survival, and in that killing is a certain pleasure that is born of necessity. There is a balance in my life and in the life around me that is disrupted by the beliefs on the other side of the road.

"I know how to identify my territory, my boundaries, and to make those boundaries clear to others. I also know that I cannot survive, and my family cannot thrive unless I mark my territory well and patrol it. I am here to teach you about that, about setting the limits you need to thrive in your own life."

Forever after, Mountain Lion was my teacher on the subject of personal boundaries, something that until then I'd had a great deal of trouble understanding. I have fully incorporated his character in my mind, to the extent that whenever I am feeling overwhelmed by others, or feel that others are not respecting my limits, I can immediately call up the image of Mountain Lion and begin a problem-solving dialogue with him.

It was interesting to me that even though the Mountain Lion took on a personal history that I found intriguing, the other fetiches seemed to resist him for a long time. It really seemed as though they made him prove himself before they accepted him.

I use my six fetiches in a conference framework, organized around what the native Americans call a

Medicine Wheel. The following describes how the Medicine Wheel works.

■

THE DYNAMICS OF THE MEDICINE WHEEL

Variations of Medicine Wheels have been found in ancient societies throughout the world. In his book *The Way Of The Shaman,* Michael Harner suggests that it may have evolved in many cultures, in various parts of the globe, not because it was communicated from tribe to tribe, but because it served a universal need and was developed by trial and error, more or less in the same period, throughout the world.

In the model of the Medicine Wheel that I use, there are four spokes, or quadrants, representing the four compass directions—North, South, East and West. Each of these is also assigned a human trait: North is knowledge, South is innocence, East is illumination, and West is introspection.

Those who developed this wheel believed that one became *whole,* that is, one understood and was successful in life, only when he or she had developed the use of all four of these traits. In this respect, the wheel serves as the model for a fully functioning, or fully mature or enlightened self.

I place the fetiches around the Medicine Wheel according to what I feel at that moment each one best represents. For example, Coyote is placed at the south; even though he is knowledgeable (North). The greatest lesson he has to teach is Innocence, or the ability to stay "open" and not be controlled by one's knowledge. Bird, on the other hand, clearly belongs on the East, since his way is one of Illumination. Most of my fetiches have a particular place on the wheel that do not change over time. Others seem to change their places, never taking the same place twice in a row. And still others reflect strengths associated with one or more positions. For example, Spirit Bear is intuitive and knowledgeable in approximately equal degrees.

If all the four quadrants of your Medicine Wheel aren't filled, that is, if you don't have a fetich that represents the traits of each compass direction, there are a couple of things to look at. First, are you choosing only fetiches that are a mirror image of you? If that is the case, look carefully at this fact. What trait do they emphasize? Is that trait your own strongest or your own weakest personal trait? Then look for at least one fetich that represents the antipodal position: for example, if your fetiches are all North, or Knowledge fetiches, look for one that would be a South, or Innocence fetich for you. If you have only one trait not covered, on the other hand, don't worry about it. Other fetiches, though maybe not predominantly representing that trait, will collectively fill in; two fetiches with secondary strengths in that trait often prove to be at least as effective as one for whom it is a primary strength. One of the great beauties of the Medicine Wheel is that there is a cumulative strength, wherein the total is exponentially greater than the sum of the parts.

Where do you place a fetich that appears to have strengths in two, three, or even all four of the quadrants? Pick the place where you need him or her the most. If you know your fetich well, you will not forget that it has talents or strengths in all four quadrants.

■

STARTING PLACES After I have placed the fetiches in the circle or Medicine Wheel, I decide where I should place myself. There is, in Northern Cheyenne thought, the idea that we each have a Starting Place at the wheel. The starting place is determined by our God-given talents, that is, the particular gift we brought into the world with us at our birth. The Starting Place for a person who is born highly intuitive, for example, would be on the Eastern quadrant. A person who has the gift of introspection would have a starting place on the Western quadrant, and so forth.

Starting Places are important to acknowledge and identify not only because they are where we find the greatest source of self-power in our own lives, but because that is where we find the greatest source of self-power in others. Knowing our Starting Places also helps us recognize what we must learn from life, or find in a helper, to be whole, that is, to experience the fullest potentials of our own lives. We can identify what it is we want to learn for ourselves, and what things we need in our lives that we will have to depend on others to provide.

Every person at the Medicine Wheel is valued equally, none more or less than any other. The reason for this is simple. No one comes into life whole. All of us are "learners." And very few people, the Native Americans believed, leave the world whole. We sit at the wheel as equals because by doing so we are able to share in our collective gifts, or Starting Places. Here's how that works:

As a number of people sit at a wheel, sharing their

thoughts, feelings, ideas, or simply meditating together, each person experiences the *wholeness* made possible by their coming together. The person who is strong in knowledge but weak in introspection gains strength through the introspection brought to the wheel by another person or persons. And those who might be strong in other ways but weak in knowledge find wholeness through him.

Taking part in this wholeness is known as "turning the wheel." The image I like to use here is that of several people sitting in a circle, and as the wheel turns the traits from everywhere around the circle form a swirl of solid energy that flows into each participant. This swirl of energy is a blending of all the gifts brought to the wheel by its participants.

■

THE MEDICINE WHEEL FOR INTUITIVE PROBLEM-SOLVING

When I work with my fetiches to address a particular problem, I begin the Medicine Wheel, or conference, by taking a position according to how I am feeling about myself at that moment. I look for my strongest trait—choosing from knowledge, illumination, introspection, innocence—and take my position accordingly. Likewise I assign positions to the six fetiches, as I've described earlier.

I then deeply relax. When I am feeling comfortable and open, I present my question or problem to the fetiches, asking them, for example: "I am having trouble seeing the inner resources of a particular client. I would like help seeing into him."

Still deeply relaxed, I wait for an answer. Sometimes I look from one fetich to another randomly, until one begins to talk with me. Sometimes I ask a fetich a question, such as, "What can you tell me about this problem?" Sometimes I am instantly drawn to one fetich or another. I allow myself the luxury of following whatever happens.

In most fetich conferences, or Medicine Wheels, I will talk with every fetich, and in doing so it is not unusual to get several slightly different perspectives on whatever problem I am working on. Sometimes the opinions of the fetiches are contradictory. This can, or course, be confusing, but usually the varied perspectives expand the way I look at things.

■

THE WHEEL OF CONTRADICTION

Resolving contradictions in what the fetiches say is not always an easy process, but, as in life, the best decisions are ultimately made by "considering the source along with the advice." Always remember that it is rare that one fetich, working alone, would be able to present a "truth" directly, since each fetich, like each person in life, has only a piece of the truth. He is not *whole* but works only from his own Starting Place. Rather, it is the collective *voice* of the fetiches working at the Medicine Wheel that provides an answer that is whole—or anything even close to it.

An image that has always been helpful for me in this respect is one provided by the 14th century writer Geoffrey Chaucer. In a poem called "Parliament of Fowls," the Falcon has come of age and his father has asked all the birds in the kingdom to advise his son about choosing a mate. In effect, the birds form a Medicine Wheel.

Each bird, in turn, offers his advice about the traits that make the best mate: the duck says the best mates have webbed feet; the swan says the best mates have powerful wings and long graceful necks, and so on. Each participant, of course, describes the ideal mate in terms of his own image and likeness. And, in the end, the falcon wisely sees that this is so, saying that the message they have taught him is not to look for webbed feet or long necks but to look for those traits that "bringeth pleasure and are right to mine own eye."

One of the beauties of working with the fetiches at the Medicine Wheel in the way that you'll be able to do by the time you finish reading this section, is that if you follow the entire process you will have a clear picture of each fetich just as the falcon in Chaucer's poem had a clear picture of each bird. Having that picture, knowing each fetiche's personal traits, you can accurately and truly "consider the source." You will know each fetiche's interests, personal limits, blind spots and clear areas of vision, and you can measure whatever they tell you against these known things.

An excellent example of this dynamic comes to mind. A couple of years ago, I was teaching a woman to work with fetiches, and she asked them to help her decide whether or not to break up with her lover, a man she'd lived with for five years. She had four fetiches, and all but one had what she considered to be good reasons for her to stay in the relationship. The fourth fetich, a tiny ivory carving of a monkey which she had inherited from a favorite uncle, told her to get out, to go on a trip alone and when she returned tell her lover that the relationship was finished.

The woman felt uncomfortable with this advice. But because the fetich had belonged to her favorite uncle, and she had always found the information she accessed with it useful, she could not understand her ambivalence. I asked the woman to think, in a general way, about the theme of taking off for a trip in the midst of a crisis. Was that kind of behavior in any way a part of her deceased uncle's character?

"Oh, yes," she said. "He was famous for his disappearing acts whenever the going got tough."

"Did that work for him?" I asked.

She shook her head. "No, the trouble was always there when he returned—often compounded by his disappearance."

Considering the fetich in light of this, the woman disregarded the advice. It had been a part of her uncle's character that she had never admired—though there were many other aspects to his character from which she drew inspiration and strength. She stayed with her lover, and they eventually worked out their problems. She continued to work with the fetich of the ivory monkey, however, because in a great many ways the information she accessed with it was valuable. But thereafter she always went through this process of *considering the source* before she fully embraced the ideas of any of her fetiches.

■

THE FETICH AND MEDICINE WHEEL PROCESS SIMPLIFIED

Prey God Fetiche from Bureau of Ethnology Report, 1881

1. Choose each of your fetiches carefully. Choose objects to which you feel a strong personal attachment.

2. Dialogue with each fetich, so that you get to know it thoroughly.

3. Get a clear picture of the Medicine Wheel in your mind. Let the four quadrants guide you in developing a model of wholeness of your own.

4. Place the fetiches around the wheel, according to what you feel are their Starting Places.

5. Choose your own place at the wheel, according to what you feel is your Starting Place.

6. Take a moment to define the problem you wish to solve. Then address your fetiches, and start asking questions.

7. Wait for answers from your fetiches. Sit quietly. Be patient.

8. Encourage dialogue between your fetiches. For example, (To fetich X:) ''Fetich Y says that I should take the job in Los Angeles. Does this seem like a good idea to you?''

9. *Consider the source along with the advice* you get from your fetiches.

10. Tape record the work you do with your fetiches, and play back these tapes at later dates.

THE MEDICINE WHEEL

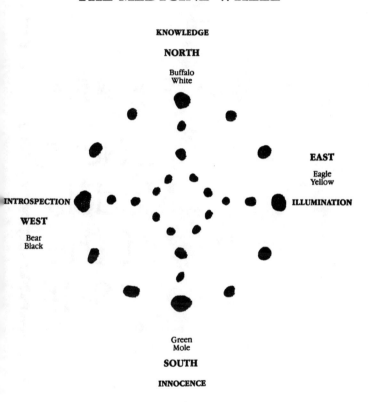

Cheyenne "Medicine Wheel"

CHAPTER FIVE:

New Models of the Self

For some people, the tools I have described in this book will represent a shift in perception, a new view of the capabilities of the self. In spite of this, these are tools intended for every day use which, with the support of the thousands of other people who are presently using these skills, will become as common as reading and writing in our society.

But let's be realistic. If you're the CEO of a large corporation you probably won't feel comfortable about bringing your fetiches with you to your next stockholders' meeting, announcing that they will help you make a decision about correcting slumping sales. However, if you are working with your fetiches on a regular basis in the privacy of your home or office, their holographic correlatives in your mind will always be present. You can turn to them whenever you wish and no one but you will be the wiser.

Some people find inner guides more "portable" and adaptable to their needs than are fetiches. I know of business people, artists, teachers, salespeople, doctors, college professors, psychotherapists, and health practitioners who never make a major decision without going into the privacy of their inner worlds to consult with their inner guides. The truth is that we probably do this automatically, maybe without even being conscious that we've done so, dozens of times each day—even though no one had ever taught us this process. Many people learning how to use inner guides for the first time have remarked that they realized, only after being shown, that they had had such guides and used them all their lives. They had just never given that process a second thought, or had never been fully conscious of what they were doing. After learning about them, their guides became more useful, since they were able to use them more by choice than by serendipity.

As you become more and more adept at using your inner resources in the ways described here, it also will become increasingly clear to you that the boundaries of the self, the influence you exert on the world, extends far beyond the immediate environment. You will begin to experience a new perception of the self, one predicted by the new physics wherein we have seen that our thoughts and feelings are subject to the same natural laws that govern the behavior of all matter and energy in the Universe. You will begin to see that your interactions with others begin not at the moment when you have entered the room where they are sitting, but at the moment when they first enter your consciousness, though that may have occurred miles away or even weeks or months before.

The more we develop tools for making full use of our inner resources, the more it becomes clear that just as our lives did not begin on the day we left our mother's wombs, so the life of an idea or feeling does not begin the moment it is born into the external environment as words or actions or "knowing glances." We affect and are affected by the activities of the inner worlds of people halfway around the Earth, or who lived their lives hundreds of years ago. And if the Theory of Relativity is as correct as scientists seem to believe it is, we are as affected by events in the future as we are by events in the immediate present or the distant past.

All this seems far removed from our daily lives, where most of our attention truly seems focused in the present. Yet these are principles which have been espoused since the beginning of recorded time, and the new physics is providing substantial evidence that they are true. How strange it sometimes seems to me that, after a long absence from our lives, the intuitive arts, as they are sometimes called, would be ushered back into our lives not by religion, their traditional escort, but by science, mid-wifed by research into the behavior of subatomic particles in laboratories the world over.

I think it is not exaggerating to say that throughout Western society we are experiencing a major shift in our understanding of the self. Throughout history humans have based their personal aspirations and their expectations for their children on social models that defined the limits and possibilities of the self. These models have never, of course, been static. Rather, they have constantly responded to human change.

A number of years ago, while researching the mental training of super-athletes, I learned how this dynamic works even in physical achievement. World's records of high-jumping, diving, running, etc., are constantly being pushed outward and upward. Until the four-minute mile was broken, it was believed that this was the outer limit of human capability. That was the model. Many people had tried to break through this barrier, but no one succeeded until Roger Bannister did it. Once that new record was clearly established in the minds of runners all over the world, that piece of the model of the self was altered forever. And with that change in the model came one person after another who could better the four-minute mile.

Why was it that practically over night, people were able to accomplish a physical feat that for centuries had been thought to be impossible? Super-athletes and their trainers say that only by examining the model of the self, rather than the physical training and conditioning, can we understand this phenomenon.

Author and teacher George Leonard shows athletes and others how to create new models of the self, based on shifting one's attention from the body as being fundamentally a physical entity to the body being fundamentally an energetic one. He uses the term "Energy Body" to describe this entity and says the human individual is to be viewed:

> ... as an energy being, a center of vibrancy, emanating waves that radiate out through space and time, waves that respond to and interact with myriad other waves. The physical body is seen as one manifestation of the total energy being, coexisting within the Energy Body. Its reality and importance is in no way denied. It provides us with the most reliable information as to the condition of the total being. The Energy Body, on the other hand, is less reliable and more difficult for us

144

to perceive at this stage in our development. But it is far less limiting than the physical body. It can change shape, size, density, intensity, and other qualities. Each of these changes influences the physical body to some extent. In some mysterious way that we can't yet fully understand, the Energy Body also seems to transcend space and time, connecting each human consciousness to all of existence.

The inner guides, visions, dreams, and fetiches are all parts of the Energy Body that Leonard describes. And as such, they do, as he says, connect us to all of existence in ways we can't yet fully comprehend.

In the work of Jesuit paleontologist Pierre de Chardin, we are asked to contemplate the possibility of a "thinking layer" that envelops the Earth, a layer in which each one of us, like one cell in a brain, makes a contribution to a whole that is too large for any one of us to comprehend fully. Chardin says:

This noosphere is just as extensive and coherent as any other sphere of our planet, be it the atmosphere, the lithosphere, the hydrosphere, or the biosphere. Outside and above the biosphere, the noosphere constitutes the thinking layer, which, since its germination at the end of the Tertiary period, has spread over and above the world of plants and animals.

The activities of our inner worlds, which we become increasingly familiar with as we work with tools such as those I describe here, are so much a part of this noosphere that at one point we must see ourselves enveloped by it entirely. In a very real way, each individual consciousness is no more separated from the Earth's noosphere than is a brain cell separated from the brain. What's more, individual consciousness merges with and emanates from the noosphere.

In struggling to appreciate fully the relationship between our inner worlds and the Earth, I have found support in the following words of Lewis Thomas:

> *We still argue the details, but it is conceded almost everywhere that we are not the masters of nature that we thought ourselves: we are as dependent on the rest of life as are the leaves or midges or fish. We are part of the system. One way to put it is that the Earth is a loosely formed, spherical organism, with all its working parts linking in symbiosis.*

It is my belief that only by gaining greater knowledge about, and skill with, the contents of our inner worlds, can we solve the chief problem of today—whether or not we will destroy our planet, render it uninhabitable by life as we know it, or fully embrace it and help it flourish. We have the technology to go either way. But the choice about how to use that power may or may not be a "rational one." Our inner world often works in mysterious ways. For example, the captains and crews of the ships that collided in the fog under the Golden Gate Bridge, ruining a twenty mile stretch of California coastline, were presumably rational people, people with good intentions. Yet, the "accident" happened, as accidents will. I think it is legitimate to say that such accidents, events that truly threaten the health of our Earth, might be averted more often than not if those in command were more familiar with their inner worlds and through that familiarity had a sense of powerful connectedness and interrelatedness with our planet.

The more familiar we become with our inner worlds, and the more we pay homage to our connectedness with the noosphere, the more we are likely to protect and love that which nurtures us, the Earth herself. And the more connected we feel, the more we will receive and enjoy the bounties of our planet.

APPENDIX

Help From Inner Guides During The Dying Process

When I was in high school back in Michigan, thirty five years ago, I was hunting in the woods near my home. I shot two rabbits and took them home for dinner that night. When I made the incision to skin the second animal, the room filled with a putrid smell.

I didn't eat either of the animals but a small cut on my hand was enough to infect me with what the doctors later diagnosed as Tuloremia. I went into a coma, and in the process I had a clear sense of having left my body. I remember being in a startlingly bright tunnel of light, passing along through it smoothly.

I looked back down the tunnel toward where my body lay, packed in ice on the hospital bed. I began to see that I had a decision to make—to live or to die. It seemed arbitrary at that moment, and I found myself quite attracted to that brilliant lighted universe at the other end of the tunnel.

Having made the decision to continue my life, I set out on a journey that I might not have chosen had I understood what I was getting myself in for. The physical stuff of me was, it appeared, badly damaged by the disease.

Over the months, sight returned, my senses straightened out and the physical world once again lost at least enough of its mystery to make it manageable. But thanks to the *rabbit's revenge,* as I now call it, I never again saw life with the same eyes.

The experience was repeated twelve years later following a motorcycle accident. Again there was the tunnel of light, the glimpse of the Infinite beyond, the choice to make between living and not living, and then the struggle back to physical health.

Ten years after that I began to ask why such experiences had been given me, for I did see both these near-death experiences as *gifts,* part of the material I was to bring into this life. At the time I came to this realization, I was working for a publisher who asked if I would be interested in editing a manuscript they had received from another author. I said I would take a look at it. It turned out to be a book on death and dying. I realized it was time to carefully examine my own experiences with death, and I took the opportunity of working on the book to do just that.

While working on the book about dying, I was also finishing up THE WELL BODY BOOK, which I was writing with Mike Samuels. I lived in Berkeley, and Mike lived in West Marin. I would commute a couple of times a week, as Mike and I did final editing on our book together.

In the drive between West Marin and Berkeley, I

began talking with what I took to be an imaginary character who appeared in my mind not unlike a character from a favorite book or movie would appear. However, this was not someone I knew from either of these sources. He introduced himself to me as Alex.

In the months of commuting between Marin and Berkeley, Alex and I had long conversations about death, many of which I recorded on a tape recorder I carried in my car. One evening as I was going through San Anselmo, Alex interrupted our conversation and said, "Stop here and visit Ann X."

I was startled by this demand. Up until then I had thought of Alex as nothing more than an intellectual foil for me. Certainly it had never occurred to me that he might be an entity separate from myself. I questioned him. "Why should I visit Ann? I haven't seen her in years."

In my Mind's Eye, Alex shrugged. In a rather amused way, he said, "Suit yourself. However, you could be of service to her. She's having a difficult time."

At last, to satisfy my own curiosity, I turned off and drove up to Ann's house. I knocked on the door, and it opened almost immediately. Ann stood in the open door and stared at me in disbelief.

"I've just been thinking about you," she said. "I even thought about calling you on the phone."

"What's going on?" I asked.

She invited me in and over coffee she told me that a mutual friend of ours had died only a few days before. He was a young man and his death had been the result of a violent and sudden accident.

"Since he died," Ann told me, "It is like he is always here, nagging at me, pulling at me, sort of the way a child does when it needs your attention. It's driving me crazy, and I don't know what to do."

Alex' purpose in my life became something quite different at that moment. He was no longer a fantasy for playing games inside my head. I asked him, "Is this why you sent me to visit Ann?"

He answered, rather matter-of-factly, that it was.

"So now what do I do?" I asked.

He gave me detailed instructions for Ann. The next time her dead friend nagged her, she should go to a quiet place, sit down, and just *be* with him: "Speak to him as though he was really there. Ask him what he wants from you. Be open to him. Give him permission to die, to leave this life and go on. Ask him if there is any unfinished business that he needs you to finish for him."

Ann said she felt like it was crazy talking to someone who was dead, but she would do it. At the very least it might make her feel better.

I left and a week after Ann called to tell me that she had done what I—actually Alex—had told her to do and it had worked. She had spoken with her dead friend and they had said goodbye to each other. She felt at peace and she was satisfied that he was at peace.

After this, Alex became a valuable inner resource for me. Through him I've learned much that I cannot imagine would have otherwise been accessible to me.

Alex has helped me with the deaths of both my parents, as well as the death of a close friend.

When I got the news that my father was dying, in

1973, Alex told me that I should go back to Michigan to be with him and that I should be his "guide," helping him in his passage from life to not-life. (The term "not-life" was Alex'. "Death," he tells me, "is the *process;* it is not what you *have* after your life is over.")

I argued with Alex about my taking the role as my father's guide, saying I knew nothing about this, that I had never been around a dying person before and I would not know what to do. He said, "On the contrary. You know a great deal about it. You've been there yourself—or at least almost there." This was, of course, in reference to the rabbit's revenge.

I asked Alex if he would help me. He said he would, but that I would have many others to assist me along the way. "How will I know who they are?" I asked.

"They'll tell you," he said, with a tone that implied that I was a complete idiot.

I wanted more direction than this from him. I asked for more details, for some kind of clue about the kind of help I would get and how I'd recognize it.

In a mysterious, Count Dracula sort of voice, with which he seemed to be mocking me, he said, "You will meet an older woman soon, who will tell you all you need to know to take the next step."

"Sure," I thought. "Very funny!" The joke—and he did treat it as a joke—didn't seem appropriate, given the circumstances.

Later that day I went down to the travel agency to pick up an airline ticket I'd ordered. I was in a dark mood as I left the agency, and as I went out the door I literally bumped into an older woman. I stepped away, apologizing, and as I did so I recognized her as the real estate sales woman who'd sold me a house a few years before.

I told her that my father was dying and I was going back to be with him.

She held up her index finger melodramatically: "You must come to my office and speak to me right now," she said, "I have something important to tell you."

I nodded. "Yes." It was as Alex had said it would be.

I went down the street with her to her office. She cancelled her appointments for the next hour and told me what she said I needed to know. Two years before this, her own father had died. She, too, had gone to be with him. It just so happened that he had died of exactly the same disease as my father's. She told me what to expect in the process, how to stay focused on the spiritual meaning of his death, how to give him comfort, even though some of the things I would see him go through would be shocking to me. The instructions were clear, at times, disturbingly graphic though later I found that they prepared me well for the reality I had to face.

As a result of the assistance I got from this woman, from Alex, and from a second inner guide who appeared to me, my father's death was an easy passage. In the hours I sat with him, my guides were always present, and the comfort they brought me, and which I was able to offer other members of the family, was profound.

Alex again served me in my role as a guide for dying people when my friend Beverly G. died. I had been visiting her in the hospice for several months, and then she appeared to be getting better and was released to go home. She was staying with her brother in Santa Clara, and she seemed to be doing well.

One afternoon I was just returning to my office from lunch and Alex said to me, "Run to your office and call Beverly. She's dying."

I didn't question him this time. I immediately did as I was told. Beverly's brother answered the phone and told me that Beverly couldn't talk to me.

"She's acting crazy," he said. "I just can't make sense of anything she's saying."

I said to her brother, "Charles, your sister is dying. Please do what I say. Sit down with her. Take her hand. Just be with her. Don't try to do anything except be with her. Do what I say."

I am not ordinarily aggressive in situations like this but I was then, and Charles did as I told him.

I asked him to hold the telephone to his sister's ear. He did this, and I said hello to Beverly. "Do you know who this is?" I asked.

"How are you doing?" I asked.

"Goodbye," she said. "Goodbye, goodbye, good-bye, goodbye."

"Where are you going?" I asked.

"To heaven," she said. "I'm going to heaven."

"That's great," I said. "You have many friends there, don't you?"

"Many friends," she said. She sighed, happily I thought. Then she said, "Oh, look at them. I see..."

She stopped in mid-sentence, then said, "Goodbye. Goodbye, Hal."

I heard the phone click. I hung up, and then immediately called back. The line was busy. I called again and again. Twenty minutes later, when her brother finally answered the phone, I learned that upon saying goodbye to me, Beverly folded her hands on her chest, smiled and said, "That was Hal. What a wonderful family I have." She closed her eyes and was gone.

Discovering The Gift

It has taken me many years to discover my "gifts of service," as Alex has described them to me. We all have these gifts: some in the spiritual realm, others in the physical. And according to Alex, it does not matter what these gifts happen to be, whether chopping wood, clerking in a store, or as a spiritual leader—all are of equal value to the Universe, none to be judged greater or more important than another.

"The *gift* each man and woman brings," Alex says, "is the important thing. The quality of the gift, not the activity that is the vehicle for expressing the gift, is the key."

When my mother died this summer, Alex was again present. My family had been through the Hospice way of dying with my father, years before, so we were more secure in what we were doing. In the two months it required, mother shared the experience of her death openly and fearlessly with us. With Alex' help, we were all able to support her in a completely conscious dying that she'd chosen. She made arrangements for her funeral, down to every last detail, choosing the coffin, how the flowers would be arranged in the slumber room, telling the minister what she did and didn't want said, calling musician friends to her bedside to discuss the music she would like them to play for her ("Nothing sappy," she told them).

By the end, nearly two hundred people, relatives and friends in the small mid-western town where she had made her home, were touched by her. They came to her, an endless parade of visitors, sometimes cramming into her crowded little apartment in the middle of town, to say their goodbyes or talk to her about death. They called her on the phone, and she called them.

Four days before she died my mother asked me to dial the phone for her, to contact friends and relatives who she knew wouldn't be able to visit her before she died. Each time she briefly told them that she was dying, that she intended to be gone in a couple of days, but before she left she wanted to thank them for their friendship over the years and to say goodbye. Without intending to she—and maybe all of us—became spiritual teachers for her community.

After her visit to my mother's bedside, one older woman said to me, "You have no idea how important your mother's work here has been to all of us oldsters. She has taught us that we have a choice about the way we are to die."

On the evening that mother died, I was holding her hand. Earlier that day she had said to me, "Where I'm going, I have an idea I can look down and kind of keep an eye on you. And if you're not doing what you're supposed to be doing with your life, I'm going to give you a little kick in the butt." She said this with a mischievous look in her eye, perhaps teasing. "I'm not sure how I'll arrange that yet, but I'll figure out a way."

"Okay," I said, laughing. "I'll remember that."

In the last moments, Alex was again present, giving me courage, giving me the words to say, comforting. I was not alone.

Mother's eyes drooped shut, and I decided that I would close mine as well. As I did a tremendous feeling of peace spread over me. I became aware of a shift of energy in the room. It was something like the way you feel when you have your eyes closed and someone enters the room. You become aware of their presence before you hear them or see them. I looked up. No one had entered. There was only mother and I.

I closed my eyes again, enjoying the tremendous peace I'd felt moments before. I was euphoric, almost as though I had taken a tranquilizer. And then there was a profound sense of being enveloped in—I cannot think of any other way to describe it—an energy field. It had no substance that I could detect, and yet it was real, almost palpable. In my mind's eye I saw it as a sepia colored essence, like a fog, that enveloped her and enveloped me.

Silently, speaking only in my mind I said, "I think it's time for you to go," addressing a mental image of my mother.

I opened my eyes. My mother was looking right at me, her eyes alert, happy. She said, "All right." Was she answering what I had only said in my mind? Was it coincidence?

"Go toward the light," I said, these words coming to me from Alex. "Go lightly. Lightly."

She turned her head slightly to the right. Her face lit up, and she uttered a little sound that was half surprise and half laughter. She spoke, and though I could not understand exactly what she was saying I got the definite impression that she was greeting someone, someone she was very pleased to see.

There followed a conversation. She spoke in a strange way, her words coming fast like a record speeded

157

up but with tones that sounded like a record played at half speed. Her face and her voice were expressive, excited, joyous. From time to time she paused, as though to listen to the person she saw, happy and profoundly interested in whatever it was he or she was telling her. Her eyes were wide, her face taut, the way a person's face is when they're listening intently, pleasantly surprised or excited by what they hear.

She and this presence I couldn't see or hear were having a wonderful time. And then it ended. She turned her eyes back to me, smiled.

"T," she said. "H...E...Q...U...I...E...T."

It took me a moment to realize what she was doing. She was spelling something out.

I puzzled over it for a moment, then putting it together said it aloud. "The Quiet."

She nodded. For a moment she struggled for breath.

"Go lightly," I said. "Go lightly. Lightly. Lightly."

In a soft, calm voice, I repeated it over and over again, holding her hand the whole time, close to her, at peace, feeling awed by the process yet feeling as though it was a common, everyday event. Nothing special. Nothing shocking or sensational. A gentle passage.

I felt her hand in mine but she was slipping away. I could feel that, the way one stands on the ground and watches an airplane go, getting smaller, becoming a dot, then a shadow, then only a slight parting in the clouds.

She was gone. Her face on the pillow, turned slightly to her left, bore an expression of profound peace. Somehow, even though the spirit had left her body, she looked radiant.

I said a little prayer, though I do not recall the words.

Realizing that my brother Paul, and perhaps others, would want to come and pay their last respects, I decided to brush mother's hair and straighten up the room. I collected the flowers that people had brought and placed them on the tables beside her bed.

In the process of straightening up mother's room, I accidentally dropped a photo of hers on the floor. As I bent down to pick it up I felt a sharp pain in my backsides. I let out a yelp and instantly dropped my pants realizing that I was being bitten by a wasp!

Even as this was happening I remembered mother's warning to me about figuring out a way to kick us in the butt if we weren't doing what we were supposed to be doing. I laughed out loud, looked up, and finding the humor in this cosmic joke, said "Come on, mother, lighten up!" The smile on her lifeless lips seemed to suggest that she was satisfied with her effort at comic relief.

My mother's grave marker bears the following epitaph: "A grateful life, a joyous passage." It tells the story well.

The last part, the joyous passage, is something that I would never have been able to help her enjoy except for the assistance I got from Alex.

AN ANNOTATED BIBLIOGRAPHY

The following books have influenced my writing of Inner Guides. I have made brief comments after each book title, telling why each was important to me, realizing that readers may wish to fill in some of the gaps which, in the interest of economy, I have left out of my own writing.

The Island, by Aldous Huxley, Harper & Row, 1962. This book, a Utopian novel, has inspired me perhaps more than any other book by this author. Huxley describes here a society where individuals draw fully from their own inner resources. It was during my third or fourth reading of this book, ten years ago, that I became interested in developing a set of "educational tools," if you will, for accessing our inner resources. Huxley's story of the Utopian society where this was done suggested to me that skills such as active imagination, visualization, meditation, inner guides, oracle systems, and others, could assist people in developing their "right brain" and other intuitive and creative potentials just as the "Three Rs" help develop their "left brain" potentials.

You Are Not The Target, by Laura Huxley, Tarcher, 1981. As in *The Island* by Aldous, this book inspired me to develop and teach techniques for more fully using our inner resources. Laura has described what she calls "recipes for living," creative visualizations, and other techniques, that show us how to make better use of the inner self, for solving both large and small life issues. Other books by Laura include *Between Heaven and Earth,* a sequel to *Target, This Timeless Moment,* in which she recounts her life with Aldous, and *One a day reason To Be Happy,* a children's book.

The Act of Will, by Roberto Assagioli, M.D., A Penguin Book, 1973. The following quote best tells why this book has been important to me: Assagioli says, "in moments of thoughtful deliberation and decisions, a *voice,* small but distinct, will sometimes make itself heard urging us to a specific course of action, a prompting which is different from that of our ordinary motives and impulses. We feel that it comes from the central core of our being...an overwhelming conviction that asserts itself irresistibly." This "small voice," while not altered, is amplified a thousand-fold by inner guides and the other methods I describe in this book.

Seven Arrows, by Hyemeyohsts Storm, Harper & Row, 1972. This book has done more than most to introduce shamanic techniques in a way that is entertaining, responsible, clear and usable in contemporary life. The message in Storm's work that I have found most valuable is that we each have a unique lens of perception, through which we see the world. Although this lens distorts what is really there, it is only by embracing and discovering the image on the lens that we fully enjoy, and allow the rest of the world to enjoy, our individualized beings. The lens is the Universe's gift to us, a gift whose full power is ultimately realized only in re-giving it. Storm shows how the gift is expressed in dreams, visions, "animal and ancestoral guides" and through stories.

Memories, Dreams, Reflections, by C.G. Jung, Vintage Books, 1973. This book contains Jung's "Septem Sermones ad Mortuos," originally self-published by the author in 1916. Jung occasionally gave copies of the Sermones to friends, and though he later described this work as a "sin of youth," both Jung himself and Jungian scholars say that it was perhaps the central vision upon which all his work, thereafter, was based. The work is prefaced as "The Seven Sermons to the Dead written by Basilides in Alexandria, the City where the East toucheth the West." Today this would be described as a channeled work, by an inner guide who continued to serve Jung throughout his life. There is an anagram at the end of this piece whose meaning Jung never disclosed and which has never been decoded. I am especially grateful to Jung for introducing concepts such as the collective unconscious and synchronicity which helped me see that we are all connected with the past and the future by universal threads that give us greater strength and greater responsibilities than most of us can quite accept or even imagine.

The Farther Reaches of Human Nature, by Abraham Maslow, published by Viking Press, 1979. Maslow's work on the peak experience and the nature of creativity made me realize, for the first time, that our greatest efforts should be directed not at "correcting" what we perceived as our personal shortcomings but at creating tools to move forward, exploring our individual uniqueness and what it has to offer. It was through Maslow's work that I first came to see that there was a difference between correcting disease and creating health, which has been the central theme of my work with Mike Samuels, M.D. over the years. In writing *Inner Guides,* I again acknowledge my debt to Maslow for providing the philosophical template for keeping the work regenerative rather than corrective.

BIBLIOGRAPHY

Ferguson, Marilyn. THE BRAIN REVOLUTION. New York: Bantam Books, 1973.

Garfield, M. L. & Grant, Jack. COMPANIONS IN SPIRIT. Berkeley, CA: Celestial Arts, 1985.

Goldberg, Philip. THE INTUITIVE EDGE. Los Angeles: Tarcher Books, 1983.

Green, Elmer & Alyce. BEYOND BIO-FEEDBACK. New York: Dell Publishing Co., 1977.

Harner, Michael. THE WAY OF THE SHAMAN. New York: Bantam Books, 1980.

Jung, C. G. MEMORIES, DREAMS, REFLECTIONS. New York: Vintage Books, 1965.

Jung, C. G. THE PORTABLE JUNG. England: Penguin Books, 1971.

Maslow, A. H. THE FARTHER REACHES OF HUMAN NATURE. New York: Viking, 1973.

Maslow, A. H. TOWARD A PSYCHOLOGY OF BEING. New York: Van Nostrand Reinhold Company, Inc., 1968.

Mindell, Arnold. WORKING WITH THE DREAM BODY. Boston: Routledge & Kegan Paul, 1983.

Oyle, Irving. THE HEALING MIND. Berkeley, CA: Celestial Arts, 1976.

Samuels, M., and Samuels, N. SEEING WITH THE MIND'S EYE. New York: Random House-Bookworks, 1975.

Sannella, Lee. KUNDALINI—PSYCHOSIS OR TRANSCENDENCE? San Francisco: H. S. Dakin Co., 1976.

Storm, H. SEVEN ARROWS. New York: Ballantine, 1974.

INDEX

About the Author

Hal Zina Bennett is the co-founder, with Susan J. Sparrow, of PATH: Inner Resources, established for the purpose of researching the intuitive arts and developing tools for accessing inner resources for health.

As a leading author in the holistic health and human potential movement, he has published more than a dozen books with major publishers, including the bestselling *Well Body Book,* co-authored with Mike Samuels, M.D.

Bennett is an inner resource instructor, offering short- and long-term individual consultations as well as group seminars.

Write the author for information about consulting services, lectures or personal appearances.

Hal Zina Bennett
P.O. Box 60655
Palo Alto, CA 94306

A Word from the Publisher

Celestial Arts publishes books in the areas of self-help, spirituality, awareness and consciousness, New Age, cookery, California Cuisine, health, and fitness. For a complete list of our publications please write for our free catalog or call (415) 524-1801. Our address is P.O. Box 7327, Berkeley, CA 94707.

Celestial Arts is a part of the total program of Ten Speed Press, publishers of career and life guidance books such as *What Color Is Your Parachute?* Ten Speed Press also publishes a distinguished line of cookbooks and books in the areas of business, reference, outdoors, house-crafts, lifestyle, and mischief. For Ten Speed's free catalog, please write or phone (415) 845-8414. Ten Speed Press, P.O. Box 7123, Berkeley, CA 94707.